Introduction to New Realism

ALSO AVAILABLE FROM BLOOMSBURY

Speculative Realism, Peter Gratton

The New Phenomenology, J. Aaron Simmons

After Finitude, Quentin Meillassoux

Introduction to New Realism

Maurizio Ferraris

Translated by Sarah De Sanctis

With a Foreword by Iain Hamilton Grant

BLOOMSBURY

LONDON • NEW DELHI • NEW YORK • SYDNEY

Bloomsbury Academic
An imprint of Bloomsbury Publishing Plc

50 Bedford Square
London
WC1B 3DP
UK

1385 Broadway
New York
NY 10018
USA

www.bloomsbury.com

BLOOMSBURY and the Diana logo are registered trademarks of Bloomsbury Publishing Plc

First published 2015

British Library Cataloguing-in-Publication Data
A catalogue record for this book is available from the British Library.

ISBN: HB: 978-1-47259-064-0
PB: 978-1-47259-594-2
ePDF: 978-1-47259-066-4
ePub: 978-1-47259-065-7

Library of Congress Cataloging-in-Publication Data
A catalog record for this book is available from the Library of Congress.

Typeset by RefineCatch Limited, Bungay, Suffolk
Printed and bound in Great Britain

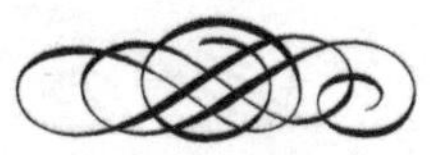

Contents

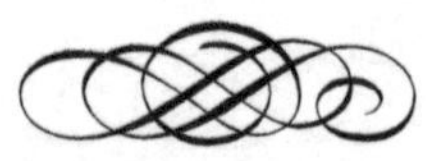

Foreword The three dogmas of transcendentalism

Iain Hamilton Grant

In the early twenty-first century, philosophy stemming from the continental tradition has become overtly realist. This does not mean it abandons the sophisticated structures of reflection for a givenness on the refutation of which its earliest moments, in Kant, were premised, just as colleagues in analytic philosophy are rediscovering these through the resurgence of German idealism. Nor does it entail a rediscovered faith in the adequacy of intellect to thing. Rather, we might say, new realisms have issued from a critique of transcendental dogmas.

In the spirit of augmenting Ferraris' fine 'Introduction' to the New Realism he has been arguing for, as he tells us, for two decades, I will provisionally characterise the most salient of these transcendental dogmas before characterising some of the experiments in removing them.

1 Only what is conceptually reconstructed can be and be known to be

This claim is foundational for transcendental philosophy insofar as it is premised not only on the analysis of knowledge claims, but on their reconstruction and application. Thus Kant, drawing on the chemical experiments of Georg Ernst Stahl, who changed 'metals into oxides and oxides back into metals',[1] argues that knowledge is not knowledge until its object has been 'made actual' *synthetically*, that is to say, until it is accommodated into the effective domain of known and knowable reality. Yet the principle is capable of further radicalisation, since once it is acknowledged that known reality is a species of constructivist practise, it is subject, as in Fichte and Levinas, McDowell and Brandom, to ethical–political governance, or is practically malleable. This leads directly to the late-twentieth-century constructivisms Ferraris characterises as proper to 'Foukant', namely, that 'reality is constructed by knowledge, knowledge is constructed by power, ergo reality is constructed by power' (see p. 24), and to the various 'linguistic idealisms' whose ontological principle is 'only what is talked about exists'.[2] Kant's late claim that 'he who would know the world must first manufacture it'[3] is the prescient motto for this confusion of epistemology and ontology. It leads to dogma 3, below.

Yet such claims are not exclusive to post-Kantian *continental* philosophy. The 'myth of the given' effectively asserts, especially under McDowell's reconstruction, that the concept of experience as preconceptually available is a contradiction in terms, since any experience recognisable as such is already rationally reconstructed. Ferraris' ingenious solution to this problem is to propose a 'naive physics' at the core of which is a revitalised *aesthesis* or philosophy of experience that resists full cognitive recovery and appears in epistemic states therefore as a negativity.

2 The primacy of the practical (the autochthonist's handbook)

The dogma concerning the primacy of the practical demonstrates that transcendentalism has no upstream, but only a downstream. This consists in the application of a finality to the reworked materials of experience and judgement under the sway of a practical reason that, because it draws its goals from what cannot be presented in experience, but only in ideas, is fully autonomous with respect to any background context or environment whatsoever. The 'autonomy' of the moral agent with respect to her 'nature' (or what is left of it, since nature is nothing other than the totality of possible experience) entails, moreover, that all acts issuing from this 'spontaneous' source share that autonomy. Having subordinated ontology to epistemology (Kant), the primacy of the practical now entails the subjugation in turn of epistemology to purpose (Fichte), so that ethics becomes 'first philosophy' (Levinas).

Again, this view is also prevalent in analytic philosophy, wherever the normativity immanent to the space of reasons undercuts any claim to 'being', 'fact' or 'really existing state of affairs'.

Its ultimate consequences are not only the autonomy of the space of reasons, but the autochthony of the subject, whose 'posits' are, for that very reason, all the reality there is ever going to be. As an afterword to this dogma, the kingdom of ends is overrun with the anarchy Kant thought to have expelled from metaphysics, only to impose it again in ethics. It is no accident that the dominant ethic of Foukant is one of 'self-construction'.

3 It is because there is thinking that there is being or, the sorceror's apprentice

This claim maximalises the first and second dogmas of transcendentalism, in that it renders human purposes into 'the cause, through one's presentations, of the actuality of the objects of those presentations'.[4] The upstream is eliminated, and the 'I think that must accompany all my representations' now becomes 'Lord of Being', or, as Ferraris renders this claim, the exclusive seat of all causality.

This claim only makes sense if we consider its converse formulation – namely, that it is because there is being that there is thinking – hopelessly false. It is *naive* to think this, insofar as it takes no account either of the motivations and practical goals of knowing, or of the insuperability of conceptual construction for representing agents (I nearly wrote 'animals'). Once, in other words, it is acknowledged that only what is can be claimed by some claimant to be, and that claimant has a right to her claim only if she has constructed that object in the first place, it follows that the claim that 'it is because there is being that there is thinking' is as good as self-refuting, insofar as that 'being' that I claim to be is first posited by me, and not given to me. The corollary of morally enhanced epistemic autochthony is an ontology restricted to artefacts, such that 'second nature' is reducibly an industrialist's paradise.

It is against these dogmas that continental realists have been labouring for the last decade or so. They are dogmas because they are unreflectively held as foundational for reflective philosophy, and it is as challenges to the limits of reflection, therefore, that continental realism may perhaps most directly be considered. My own first encounter with this strand was in the person of Manuel de Landa who, in the early 1990s, presented at a 'Virtual Futures' conference in the University of Warwick. The graduate school of which I was a member was saturated with Heidegger, postmodernism, deconstruction and various constructivisms (although these were increasingly contested by late-twentieth-century French libidinal materialism), so hearing de Landa criticising Deleuze and Guattari for their 'French-fried discourse' and generating from their 'Geology of Morals' a paper on rocks – real ones, not metaphorical ones – produced a shock almost geological in its scale and consequences. Yet in retrospect, it seems hardly surprising that the apogee of anti-realism celebrated in late-twentieth-century continental philosophy would collapse.

Amongst the more recent continental realists (as I shall call them), Quentin Meillassoux pitted what he calls the 'correlationist circle' I have characterised as the first dogma of transcendentalism, against dateable phenomena unaccompanied by thought, since *ex hypothesi* such phenomena, which Meillassoux characterises as the 'arche-fossil', predate the appearance of that being for whom appearance is an issue, and disputing thereby the claim to the universality of representing, or of being caught irretrievably in the orbit of thinking. His goal is not to eliminate correlationism, but to contextualise it, to regionalise representation in respect to being and to emphasise, in an apparently naturalist-friendly manner, the powers of mathematics with respect to what thought *does not accompany* but only *follows*, but does so both speculatively and in such a manner as meets with success.

This opens up a concern common to Ferraris, namely, the environmental thesis, according to which 'to exist is to exist in an environment' (see p. 54), or even to *resist* that environment, to stand out or against it, introducing that 'negativity' key to Ferraris' account and to which we will return below. What autonomy may be proper to knowing, therefore, is so despite its being dependent on a source of motion or causality that cannot be identified either with that knowing or with the subject who considers herself its author. In other words, despite the admirable functionality of Kant's *cogito*, to which Ferraris draws astute and considered attention in *Goodbye, Kant!*, and which does not name a thing but issues in acts, it does not exhaust the number or kind of operations that environ it. I will return to this below.

What of the naivety claim the dogmatist makes against the realist who asserts thought's dependency on being? That there are fossils (and that there were no human ones gave Kant cause for concern), does not in itself dislodge the Kantian *cogito* from its practicist throne, since although the fossil may itself predate the empirical *cogito*, it is only acknowledged as so doing if there is a *cogito* to so acknowledge it. To deny this is surely to assert those pre-conceptual givens that have been critically dispelled by the demonstration that something is given only if it is recognised as such, and since such recognition entails the activity of conceptual capacities, the 'given' is not given, but already a creature of reason.

There are really two claims here, one hard transcendentalist, the other soft. The hard transcendentalist claim is that thinking makes the object thought a *thought-object*, such that there cannot be some unconfirmable domain of unthought objects, since such objects are only limit cases for it. The second, soft transcendentalist claim is that *even if there were* non-conceptual objects or experience, or something that could be available for experience but has no commerce with the concept, this 'reality' must be alien to our conceivings of it. Accordingly, the soft transcendentalist must merely remain agnostic with respect to reality, while the hard transcendentalist has full and untrammelled access to the only reality there can be, since she is nature's author, its lawgiver and not its pupil. Once the second claim is dismantled, the first crumbles too.

This is the problem Kant's dualism of thing in itself and appearance presented to the German idealists and the critique of which was vital to its development. Reconstructing this problem in contemporary terms, Markus Gabriel has reintroduced it as an argument for a transcendental ontology he aligns with the

New Realism.[5] Starting, in good transcendentalist fashion, from the positing, the asserted positioning in some domain entailed in offering a theory of anything whatever, Gabriel argues that the condition under which this is alone possible is that what is is positing-amenable, that is, that knowledge claims are 'truth-apt'. Accordingly, the segregation of reality from the thought of reality misunderstands the reality of the thought of reality. Since a realism premised on this segregation, or, in hard transcendentalism, on its either progressive or immediate elimination (Fichte), on this account, simply does not understand what it is doing since it has failed to consistently theorise its own status in the theory it presents, the segregation cannot be maintained. Gabriel's ontology is transcendental, therefore, while his realism consists in the claim that reality contains true claims about it, and since there are as many such claims as reality affords discriminability, there are, ultimately, no true claims concerning reality as a whole, since were there such claims, they would form only the totality of facts, and a completed epistemology would be nothing more or less than the completion of a world from which positing would be absent (there are only facts), thus failing to account for world, fact, proposition or claim. It is in this realist sense, therefore, that 'the world does not exist'.[6]

Common to these realist positions is considerable investment in German idealist philosophy.[7] That philosophy has recently been rediscovered by the neo-Hegelian movement in analytic philosophy, albeit to be put largely to ends that, in accordance with the above-noted dogmas, would have to be called dogmatic insofar as it subscribes to the primacy of the practical (or normativity), eliminates nature,[8] and isolates the space of reasons from naturalist claims,[9] and thus promotes the disjunct 'science or spirit'. Ferraris draws our attention to precisely this disjunct as the outcome of a 'crisis in German idealism', which issues equally in the constructivism associated with the postmodern philosophy he characterises as belonging to 'Foukant'. This crisis, that 'all reality belongs to science, and philosophy is left with nothing much: theology, spiritualism, spiritism' (see p. 20), is not one, as naturalists might suspect, that issues from the idealists' *suspicion* of the natural sciences,[10] but rather from their *commitment* to science or *Wissenschaft*.

For the German idealists, 'science' or *Wissenschaft* is precisely the systematic order in which philosophy stands once construction achieves the aim of full autonomisation with respect to 'original being'.[11] For example, in the *Critique of Judgment*, Kant 'sacrifices'[12] the reproductive imagination, as the capacity for receiving sensible forms, in the interests of what Lyotard calls 'an aesthetics of denaturation',[13] as preparatory for the *use* to be made of nature for a finality that does not belong to it. While Lyotard proclaims this an 'ontological sacrilege'[14] and McDowell pursues a 'partial re-enchantment' of nature[15] (tidily confirming the 'science or myth' option Ferraris views the heirs of this crisis as facing), Schelling, two hundred years earlier, is a more direct critic of the dogmas of transcendentalism, deploring the merely 'economic-teleological use' made of nature by transcendental philosophy.[16]

This 'science', although here used in the specific sense the German idealists gave it, is more widespread than might first appear. Wherever, that is, a *posit* enjoys priority over the upstream and downstream of its environment, i.e. wherever rational reconstruction holds sway, 'science' leaves only myth behind it. Thus Quine considers physical objects only a 'particularly efficacious' myth, or a 'device for working a manageable structure into the flux of experience'.[17]

Amongst the elements specifically treated by German idealist 'science' is the philosophy of nature. According to the thesis that the subject does not have a monopoly on causal powers, there are positions that are not posits, but rather operations the iterations of which are precisely constitutive of whatever positings subsequently issue from it. As Schelling puts it, 'what thinks in me is what is outside me'.[18] Since thinking is not reducibly the property of the subject that partially experiences it, because the motions that give rise to it, while not yet thought, are amongst the productions of nature, nature-philosophy opens another avenue for contemporary realism insofar as it rejects deflationary for inflationary naturalism, affirms the environmental thesis Ferraris proposes in what follows, and rejects the crisis of German idealist science.

Is it along these lines that we should interpret Ferraris' offer of a 'naive physics'? Three elements of the following text tempt me to think so. Firstly, the environmental thesis itself applies to the ideal of science in German idealism: the *system*. As Schelling affirms, a system is one just when it is environed by another.[19] Thus, in terms of Ferraris' environmental ontology, 'to exist is to exist in an environment':[20] a system, that is, exists, just when it does so in an environment. Of course, the extent of a system, if truly systematic, is difficult to define insofar as nothing can be left out,[21] so that the environment of a system will itself be a system. Ultimately, however, if the system is contingent, as is the system of the world or nature, then the environment within which system exists will entail its own inexistence. Secondly, Ferraris historically associates New Realism with, inter alia, Schelling's positive philosophy. Thirdly, he is overt about the 'Hegelian' structure of the ensuing work and, as part of this Hegelian structure, there is the question of *negativity*, to which I now turn.

While for Hegel negativity will always be recovered in positivity, or in the fleshing out of reason's self-understanding, for Ferraris, the negative will be affirmed as positive not in the sense of understanding, but precisely as the environmental ontology, while remaining negative for epistemology. 'Naive physics' is precisely the lever by which that confusion of ontology and epistemology from which contemporary philosophy suffers, is sundered. Epistemology, firstly, is resisted by the naive physics attendant upon the full range of aesthesis or perception, not all of which is articulated when understood, as is primarily evident when experience, rather than confirming an epistemic claim, resists it. The consequent revelation of unamendability thus becomes the surd-like, 'irreducible remainder' that furnishes the environment against which what exists does so.

Negativity has, however, another register than the overtly German idealist one. This concerns the trap that objects set for realists. A realism that asserted that, to avoid over-subjectivising reality, turn immediately to the object, would not merely be naive in the modest sense Ferraris gives the term here, but also in the transcendental sense. Negativity, that is, entails that realism cannot be accommodated by what Gabriel calls a 'naïve ontology of individual things'.[22] To see why, consider the early-twentieth-century idealist philosopher Bernard Bosanquet's proposals for alliance with the 'neo-Realists' of his age. These latter are so called because they assert the mind-independence or physical reality of sensa against their idealist colleagues who assert the reality of thought. But in so doing, Bosanquet argues, they over-emphasise one class of reals at the expense of reality itself. In a fine definition of realism's fundamental indifference to objects, Bosanquet writes: 'everything is real so long as we do not take it for more than it is'.[23] No sooner is one a realist about *x* than one must contrastively be an 'unrealist' about not-*x*. This is why the New Realism is not a realism concerning this or that thing or set of things, but why it must also be a realism concerning negativity: the fundamental ontological unit is not the thing, but the environment or field against which what is exists. And this is also why, in the end, there is nothing particularly naive about the post-transcendentalist deployment of a physics as capable of addressing the artefacts environing the eminently constructible social domain and the unamendable remainder that cannot be resolved into reason.

The point of the critique of the dogmas of transcendentalism is not that construction does not obtain, nor that Foukant does not exist; indeed, negativity is reality's deconstruction of reason, just as naive physics forms systems. In consequence, neither reality nor ideality suffers elimination, and philosophy retains both its dignity and its essential task – the knowing, as far as is possible (or 'in accordance with power', according to Plato), of what is.

It is one of the inherently refreshing aspects of reading Ferraris' book that the dogmas of transcendentalism, no less than those of naturalism and normativism, are cast aside and the doors opened once again onto a broader philosophical field than the courthouse, the battlefield or the debating chamber. These passages are opened by way of philosophical experiments in bypassing those dogmas. The task of philosophical invention is not marginal to the discipline, but constitutive of it. But it is inherently tied, if philosophy is doing its job at all, not only to some isolable world of thought, but to the vast reality from which it issues, and with which it will never catch up, just if something exists.

References

Benoist, J., 'Reality', *Meta: Research in Hermeneutics, Phenomenology and Practical Philosophy*, Special Issue on New Realism, 2014, 21–27.

Bosanquet, Bernard, *The Meeting of Extremes in Contemporary Philosophy*, London: Macmillan, 1923.

Bosanquet, Bernard, *The Principle of Individuality and Value*, London: Macmillan, 1912.

Dennett, D., 'The evolution of why', available at http://ase.tufts.edu/cogstud/dennett/papers/Brandom.pdf.

Ferraris, M., 'New Realism as Positive Realism', *Meta: Research in Hermeneutics, Phenomenology and Practical Philosophy*, Special Issue on New Realism, 2014, 172–213.

Ferraris, M., 'Sum ergo cogito. Schelling and the positive realism', in Emilio Carlo Corriero and Andrea Dezi, eds, *Nature and Realism in Schelling's Philosophy*, Turin: Accademia University Press, 2014.

Ferraris, M., *Goodbye, Kant!*, trans. Richard Davies, Albany, NY: SUNY Press, 2013.

Franks, P.W., *All or Nothing. Systematicity, Transcendental Arguments and German Idealism*, Cambridge, MA: Harvard University Press, 1995.

Gabriel, M., 'Is Heidegger's 'turn' a realist project?', *Meta: Research in Hermeneutics, Phenomenology and Practical Philosophy*, Special Issue on New Realism, 2014, 44–73.

Gabriel, M., *Der Mensch in Mythos. Untersuchungen über Ontotheologie, Anthropologie und Selbstbewusststeinsgeschichte in Schellings 'Philosophie der Mythologie'*, Berlin: De Gruyter, 2006.

Gabriel, M., *Fields of Sense*, Edinburgh: Edinburgh University Press, 2014.

Gabriel, M., *Transcendental Ontology. Essays in German Idealism*, London: Bloomsbury, 2011.

Gabriel, M., *Warum es die Welt nicht gibt*, Berlin: Ullstein, 2013.

Grant, Ian Hamilton, *Philosophies of Nature after Schelling*, London: Continuum, 2008.

Hacking, Ian, *The Social Construction of What?* Cambridge, MA: Harvard University Press, 1999.

Kant, Immanuel, *Critique of Pure Reason*, trans. Norman Kemp Smith, London: Macmillan, 1929.

Kant, Immanuel, *Critique of Judgment*, Ak V: 177n, trans. Werner S. Pluhar, Indianapolis, IN: Hackett, 1987.

Kant, Immanuel, *Opus postumum*, trans and ed. Eckart Förster, Cambridge: Cambridge University Press, 1993.

Lyotard, Jean-François, *Leçons sur l'analytique du sublime*, Paris: Galilée, 1991.

McDowell, J., in Nicholas H. Smith, ed. *Reading McDowell on Mind and World*, London: Routledge, 2002.

McDowell, J., *Mind and World*, Cambridge, MA: Harvard University Press, 1996.

Meillassoux, Q., *After Finitude*, London: Continuum, 2008.

Putnam, H., 'How to be a sophisticated "naïve realist"', in M. De Caro and D. Macarthur, eds, *Philosophy in an Age of Science*, Cambridge, MA: Harvard University Press, 2012.

Quine, W.V.O., 'Two dogmas of empiricism', in W.V.O. Quine, *From a Logical Point of View*, Cambridge, MA: Harvard University Press, 1963, 20–46.

Schelling, F.W.J., 'Darlegung des wahren Verhältnisses der Naturphilosophie zur verbesserten Fichteschen Lehre', in *Schellings Werke*, ed. K.F.A. Schelling, Stuttgart and Augsburg: Cotta, 1856–61.

Schelling, F.W.J., 'Stuttgart seminars', in Thomas Pfau, ed. and trans. *Idealism and the Endgame of Theory. Three Essays by F.W.J. Schelling*, Albany, NY: SUNY Press, 1994.

Schelling, F.W.J., *First Outline of a System of Naturephilosophy*, trans. Keith R. Peterson, Albany, NY: SUNY Press, 2003.

Schelling, F.W.J., *System der Weltalter*, ed. Siegbert Peetz, Frankfurt: Klostermann, 1998.

Scott Scribner, F., *Matters of Spirit. J.G. Fichte and the Technological Imagination*, Pennsylvania, PA: Pennsylvania State University Press, 2010.

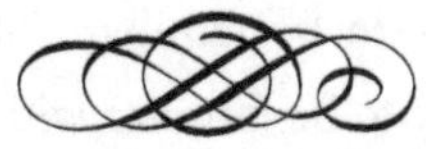

A few introductory remarks

Back to reality

In 2006, the French philosopher Quentin Meillassoux published what is arguably one of the most debated books of the past few years: *Après la finitude. Essai sur la nécessité de la contingence.*[1] In it, he set himself against all the philosophy that preceded him, accusing it of 'correlationalism': for too long philosophers have posited that humans have only ever access to the *correlation* between thought and being, but never to being itself. It was time to go back to the absolute: it was time to go back to reality.

Two years later, a very influential movement was born: that of Speculative Realism, encompassing Graham Harman, Iain Hamilton Grant, Ray Brassier and Meillassoux himself. Although these thinkers have very different positions, they all share the wish to go beyond correlation and reach the 'in-itself' that post-Kantian philosophy had seemingly forsaken – at least in the continental tradition.

The reader is likely to be familiar with these perspectives. What they are unlikely to be familiar with is the counterpart of speculative realism that has been taking place in Italy for two decades now. I have to say that I have been mostly alone in my realist battle, of which the first signs date back as early as 1997 in my *Estetica razionale*.[2] What follows is the summary of my own realist position, as I have developed it in several books during the past twenty years, which have only recently started to be translated into English.[3]

As I will argue in the pages to come, my own realism is part of a wider *realist turn* that has taken over continental philosophy in the past decades. For an in-depth analysis of the relationship between my perspective and some of the other main advocates of the return to reality, I refer the reader to the Afterword of the present volume.

2011

New realism is one of the very few philosophical movements of which one may indicate the exact date and place of birth:[4] it was 23 June 2011 at 13.30 at the restaurant 'Al Vinacciolo' in Via Gennaro Serra 29, Naples. I can be so accurate because I was there, with Markus Gabriel and his Italian collaborator Simone Maestrone, after a seminar at the Italian Institute for Philosophical Studies. Markus was in the process of founding an international centre of philosophy in Bonn and wanted to inaugurate it with a big conference. I told him that the right title would be 'New

Realism'. I thought that name captured what in my opinion was the fundamental character of contemporary philosophy: that is, a certain weariness of postmodernism and the belief that everything is constructed by language, conceptual schemes and the media. Well, it is not like that: something, or rather, much more than we are willing to admit, is not constructed – and this is a wonderful thing, otherwise we could not distinguish dreams from reality. I announced the conference a few weeks later, in an article published in *La Repubblica* on 8 August 2011, and since then the debate has never ceased, both in Italy and abroad,[5] producing several contributions – including many of my writings on the subject,[6] the books by Markus Gabriel[7] and that by Mauricio Beuchot and José Luis Jerez.[8]

Some people, with incurable optimism (because a newspaper article would never be enough to trigger a debate of this magnitude), argued that it was all just media hype. Of course, so much interest has surprised even me – and I had held a realistic position for twenty years at that point,[9] without this giving rise to much sensation. But evidently it was time for a change of paradigm. On 8 August – that is, precisely the day when the term 'New Realism' was made official in my article in *La Repubblica* – I was at the airport in Athens and I began to receive a flood of text messages and emails, as if that name had captured a feature of what is vaguely called the 'spirit of the age'. In a near-perfect coincidence, on 7 August 2013, at the World Congress of Philosophy, Umberto Eco's lecture on old and new realism was presented – and it is hard to believe that Eco (who has been a realist for decades) could be the kind of person that easily gives in to media suggestions.

So, as I am now writing, two years and a few months have passed since the start of the debate. What is more, it has been twenty years since I had a banal and yet crucial epiphany. I was in Naples, in the same place that had witnessed the baptism of new realism, and I opened a conference by Hans-Georg Gadamer, an affable *grand seigneur*, who explained that 'being that can be understood is language'. I said to myself: this conference, of course, is language. And even the books I have read and written are language. But is Vesuvius, out there, language? And, more seriously, why should we reduce being to understanding? The question of Vesuvius challenged another one of my great teachers, Jacques Derrida, who had argued that 'there is nothing outside the text'. But there was another issue that, I think, was more Derridean than ever: there can be ontology without transparency: indeed, a certain opacity seems to be the fundamental nature of all that exists. I think these two decades of realism have been, for me, the attempt to find an answer to these two questions.

1983–2013

I consider it a special privilege to have participated in both seasons, that of weak thought,[10] which dates back to 1983, and that of new realism, today. And I see no contradiction in this. I challenge anyone to find in my early writings a defence of the thesis that 'there are no facts, only interpretations', or 'there is nothing outside the text' or 'being that can be understood is language'. My position has always been realist.[11] I rejected

Gadamer's antirealism, because it regarded dialogue as a creator of consensus; and I did so through Derrida – whose deconstructive fury I nevertheless criticised, since it was counterbalanced through his unique style, but became grotesque when used by his imitators. As for Vattimo, he has never been a theoretical model for me, but always and only an important stylistic model, since he showed me the importance of writing clearly and without circumlocutions as well as the need for a certain irony, saving me from imitating Derrida. I do not think I have ever shared one of his theses, nor would he have ever expected me to do so. Philosophy is not like psychoanalysis, and it is not necessary to share the same theories on libido in order to collaborate.

The only thing that has changed since then is that, while I initially hoped that a little antirealism could contribute to achieve emancipation, I realised that the opposite is true. So I began to think that antirealist positions are actually inappropriate, from a political standpoint. Also, I asked myself (but this is yet another question) why philosophy should not talk about perception but always and only about interpretations, as if people did not perceive but only interpreted, and as if philosophy had any extra know-how with respect to interpretations and ignored everything about perception instead. At the time of Aristotle it was considered normal for a philosopher to speak of physics, hermeneutics and perception. Now it seems obvious that I should not write on physics (which is understandable), but it seems equally obvious that I should not write a perceptology – which is inexplicable, since Husserl and Merleau-Ponty did.

What I find the most inexplicable is why a philosopher should be, as such, an expert in interpretations. If someone admits they know nothing about physics and dares not speak of perception, why should they declare themself an expert in interpretations? As for those who rightly regard it as trivial to reduce their philosophical activity to the assertion 'there are perceptions', it seems rather odd that they should find it somehow relevant to practice a philosophical activity whose core is reduced to the assertion 'there are interpretations' (which is what actually happened in the postmodern era). But more on this later.

New realism

Leaving autobiographical information aside, let me now get to new realism. New realism is a critique of constructivism, running parallel to many other movements in contemporary philosophy that do the same, such as, in particular, speculative realism.[12] From this point of view, it implies a critique not only of postmodernism but also of the philosophy of the last two centuries in general. As we shall see, I believe philosophical thought has been marked by confusion between ontology (what there is) and epistemology (what we know, or think we know, about what there is). Now, rather than merely criticising postmodernism and its philosophical antecedents, new realism tries to render their claims pertinent. There are areas of being that are, in fact, socially constructed: for example, there are social objects, such as philosophical movements like postmodernism or new realism.

But there are other areas of being that are *not* socially constructed, for instance natural objects (such as postmodernists and new realists taken as living human bodies).

Obviously, there is much social construction that enters the physical life of new realists no less than postmodernists. However, arguing that the heartbeat or respiration of new realists and postmodernists is socially constructed, or perhaps that the heartbeat or respiration of postmodernists is socially constructed and those of new realists are not, seems to me to be nonsensical. Yet when my teacher Derrida wrote 'there is nothing outside the text' he implied that even heartbeat and breathing are socially constructed. Such a thesis is excessive and means everything and nothing, exposing one to easy criticism.

Whereas if we say that 'there is nothing *social* outside the text' we say something that illuminates the functioning of the social world. For example, if there were no texts there would be neither postmodernism nor new realism – and it would not be a tragedy – but there would not even be bank accounts, fees, pensions, promises or holidays. In short, there would not be many important things. Saying that 'there is nothing social outside the text' means highlighting a distinctive feature of the social world, explaining why documents are so important – in fact, the greatest technological innovations of the past few decades, i.e. computers and mobile phones, are essentially meant for the production of documents. This is a process that Derrida had sensed with dowsing and prophetic lucidity. Who else, at the time when the end of writing was being proclaimed, could have written that writing was going to boom and take over the world?[13]

But all of this goes to waste in a statement as easy to attack as 'there is nothing outside the text'.

New realism is the name of a broad transformation that took place in contemporary philosophical culture and that was later developed in many directions and under different labels. First of all, there was the *end of the linguistic turn* as well as a stronger realist inclination on the part of philosophers who, while not adhering to postmodernist positions, had previously been more open to constructivism and the idea that conceptual schemes frame our experience. Think of Hilary Putnam's passage from 'internal realism' to 'common-sense realism',[14] or of the reassertion of the importance of experience in Umberto Eco.[15] Another way in which the turn took place is through the *return to perception*, that is, to a kind of experience traditionally neglected by the philosophical transcendentalism that culminated in postmodernism. Typically, the fact that aesthetics returned to be considered not as a philosophy of illusion but as a philosophy of perception[16] revealed a new openness towards the external world, namely a real that lies beyond conceptual schemes and that is independent from them – i.e. the real that makes it is impossible for us to correct optical illusions or change the colour of the objects surrounding us by means of mere reflection.

A third significant element of the realist transformation is what I would call the *ontological turn*, namely the fact that both in analytic and in continental philosophy there has been an increasing relaunch of ontology as the science of being[17] and of the multiplicity of objects,[18] which – from perception to society – constitute a research area that is not necessarily subordinated to natural science. With the return of ontology, therefore, there was the overcoming of the prevailing philosophical attitude since Kant, who had bid ontology farewell by claiming that philosophy had to cease dealing with objects (pertinent to science) and give up the 'proud name of an ontology' so as to merely investigate – under 'the modest title of analytic of the pure understanding'[19] – the conditions of possibility of knowing these objects (namely, it had to set itself either in favour of or against science).

From a historical perspective, new realism can be inserted into a long genealogy that goes back to Schelling's 'positive philosophy'[20] and, even before that – to give a broad idea – to Aristotle criticising Plato, to Brentano and to nineteenth-century Austrian anti-Kantism in general, to Moore's defence of common sense and, as regards my specific conception, to Paolo Bozzi's 'naive realism'.[21] In this sense, new realism is not an appeal to primitivism: on the contrary, it is very much aware of coming after postmodernism, and has internalised the latter's criticism of classical realism. In a way, new realism is intrinsically deconstructive: I have a Derridean education myself. I grew up in the hermeneutics of suspicion and in deconstruction. Then, at one point, I asked myself what was truly deconstructive and critical: to 'radicalise' Derrida, as was always done, so that if he wrote that there is nothing outside the text, we had to conclude that squirrels are socially constructed? Or to look for the area to which that statement is truly pertinent – namely, for me, the social world – without giving in to statements that disqualify the greatness and importance of Derrida's thought?

For me, there is a fundamental continuity between the project of 'reconstructing deconstruction' that I formulated a few years ago[22] and new realism. We must certainly maintain the – originally postmodern and deconstructive – criticism of the naive theory of truth as correspondence, for which the world offers itself 'as such', with no intervention of our conceptual schemes, perceptive apparatuses and cultural biases. Yet we cannot be contented with this transcendentalist common sense either (and here I believe we are not denying deconstruction, but rather performing an intimately deconstructive act). The world's resistance against our expectations and the surprises it holds for us seem to be excellent arguments proving that there is an ontological reality independent from any epistemological construction. In short, since we live in an intimately deconstructive reality, I believe there is nothing more deconstructive than realism.

One last and notable aim of new realism is the aspiration (shared by many research areas both in analytic and in continental philosophy) to overcome the internal divisions in philosophy by reaching the formulation of a 'globalised philosophy'.[23] In my view, such philosophy – constitutionally bilingual, writing both in the national language and in English, and therefore objectively richer than the English monolingualism or than the fragmentation of national languages alone – could arise at the confluence of three points:

1 *Scientific* expertise, which, in the case of a discipline with strong humanistic components such as philosophy, also means philological and historical expertise (do not forget

that these skills are increasingly rare and valuable in the context of the overall lowering of the level of education).

2 *Theoretical* competence, where the analytic (or academic) element provides the form, while the continental (or extra-academic) element provides the content. If there is one area where the saying 'concepts without intuitions are empty, intuitions without concepts are blind'[24] fully applies, it is the sphere of analytic-continental relationships.

3 *Public* relevance. People are willing to accept a technical and even impossibly difficult language if what is at stake is the treatment of cancer. But this is not what philosophy can offer. So, I believe that the capacity to address a large audience, delivering technically elaborated results in a linguistically accessible form, is inherently and not accidentally part of what philosophy should do.

Hegel

There is one last preliminary observation to be made about this book, which constitutes a synthesis of my whole philosophy. Realism, just as idealism, empiricism or scepticism, is a constant theme in philosophy. New realism, instead, is a reoccurring function: the reaction to a previous antirealist hegemony. It was so in the case of American New Realism last century,[25] with Brazilian Novo Realismo thirty-five years ago[26] and it is so in the case of new realism today. That this should happen in Europe, where postmodernism has been most influential, is not coincidental. New realists come from continental philosophy, where the weight of antirealism was far greater than in analytic philosophy.[27] Both traditions shared a premise: there is not a 'thing-in-itself', but only phenomena mediated (or created) by our conceptual schemes and perceptual apparatuses, and this is how both traditions have been affected by a 'linguistic turn'. But the linguistic turn was the result of a *conceptual* turn, characterised by a prevalence of concepts in the construction of experience[28] (and not, as it would be entirely reasonable to posit, in the *reconstruction* of experience, in scientific or philosophical description).

I would like to illustrate the new realist perspective by articulating three fundamental theses. The first, 'negativity', is a critique of the postmodern idea that the world is constructed by our conceptual schemes, all the more so as we have entered the age of immateriality and virtuality. I place this first part of my discourse under the title of 'negativity' because with postmodernism there was the triumph of negative thinking: it was posited that the world is nothing in itself, and if it is something, this essentially depends on our thoughts and our interpretations. The second thesis, 'positivity', proposes the fundamental ontological assertion of new realism, namely that not only (as acknowledged by every realist and, in many cases, even by some antirealists[29]) are there parts of reality that are independent of thought, but these parts are also able to act causally over thought and the human world. Finally, the third thesis, 'normativity', applies new realism to the sphere of the social world.

The Hegelian character of this triad is quite manifest: from the pure negativity of thought that attempts to construct the real, to the positivity of reality that feeds the mind, up until the forms of reality created by thought that become capable of making rules, and thus also negativity and prohibitions. Yes, it is Hegelian indeed. One must have models in life, after all.

Part One

Negativity

Philosophy and culture over the past two centuries (at least), and with a process that culminated in postmodernism, have been full of negativity. The basic idea that has characterised the modern and the postmodern ages was the sacrosanct belief that many things in the historical, social and political world are constructed and therefore can and should be deconstructed, criticised and transformed. Here indeed we witnessed the triumph of the ever-denying spirit: it gave us parliamentary democracy, modern science, gender equality and so on – in addition, of course, to disasters of all kinds. This negativity, however, triggered an uncontrollable process, and in particular the idea that *everything*, including lakes and mountains, is socially constructed. Such an idea surely feeds the will to power of individuals, who become, so to speak, constructors of worlds. But at the same time it presents itself as the way to a false emancipation, in which everyone can (apparently) do what they want and in which the difference between truth and fiction has ceased to exist. It is the world of what I call 'realitism' (a word modelled on the basis of 'reality shows') and that seems to best embody the spirit of postmodernism.[1]

Postmodernism

Schopenhauer's principle that 'the world is my representation' became the fundamental ontological principle of postmodernity and of the media system, which came to be considered (this is a characteristic trait of that age) as equivalent or concurrent entities. In the end, this was the true great postmodern theory: reality is constructed and therefore, ultimately, reality does not exist independently from the representations of an unspecified mankind.[2] This theory explains the hyper-enhancement of the media in postmodernity: postmodernism indeed regards itself as a philosophy of history that declares the end of reality, which was replaced by media 'fictionalisation'. If, following Nietzsche, the real world has become a fairy tale and there are no facts, only interpretations, then mediology becomes ontology and the media turn into the constructors of reality – in agreement not only with Baudrillard, who regarded the Gulf War as a pure media invention,[3] but also with Karl Rove,[4] who famously believed that imperial power is capable of constructing reality exactly as a film factory does.

This principle is articulated in the three crucial points in which I propose we summarise the postmodern *koiné*.[5] First, *ironisation*, according to which taking a theory seriously (or even just the literal meaning of words) shows a form of dogmatism and we should therefore maintain an ironical detachment from our statements – expressed typographically by inverted commas, and even physically by flexing fingers to denote quotes in oral speech.[6] Second, *desublimation*, namely the idea that desire constitutes as such a form of emancipation, because reason and intellect are forms of dominion, and liberation must be looked for through feelings and the body, which are revolutionary per se.[7] And, most of all, *deobjectification*, namely the assumption that there are no facts but only interpretations, as well as its corollary for which friendly solidarity should prevail over an indifferent and violent objectivity.[8]

It is here that we find the roots of what I propose we call the 'professional antirealism' of the humanities and philosophy. Being a philosopher at a time when the whole sphere of reality and objectivity seems covered by natural sciences (but we can very well call it 'science' *tout court*)[9] means saying that reality does not exist, that it is socially constructed, determined by language, manufactured by paradigms and so on. Thus the humanities acquire some respectability in an age of science: scientists construct, humanists deconstruct. There are three basic options: the deconstructive antirealist, the (realist or constructionist) adherent of scientism and the negative realist (for whom truth and reality are a prerogative of science).[10]

In my opinion, it is worth asking ourselves why intelligent people (as postmodern philosophers were) should be contented with saying *boutades* or exaggerations, without there being a counterpart of truth, practising what Rorty – who in my opinion was less ingenious than Foucault, Derrida and Deleuze, but is the only one who has tried to give a theoretical form to postmodern paradoxes – has rightly called 'ironic theory'. I think the reason is the one I am trying to suggest: for two centuries now philosophy has been able to choose between being subordinated to science (positivism, but think also of the craze of 'human sciences' thirty years ago) or criticising science. Since both scientists and antiscientists are convinced that knowledge of reality is the prerogative of science (the members of both categories go to the doctor if they are sick), antiscientists become antirealists as well, saying that man is a recent invention, that there is nothing outside the text and so on. Perhaps the best strategy one can adopt for criticising them is to take them seriously: 'If you say that man is a recent invention, you must tell me why you think Aristotle was not a man. If you say that there is nothing outside the text, show me the text in which you are existing in this moment.' I believe that this is the only way to avoid 'a fistfight with the fog', to borrow the expression used by Putnam.

I do not think this is a futile exercise, because it allows us to understand that postmodernism is the terminal stage (remember when there was great talk of the 'death of philosophy'?) of a crisis in German Idealism. All reality belongs to science, and philosophy is left with nothing much: theology, spiritualism, spiritism; personal lacerations, the human world, the world of life; exercises *sur place* like the overcoming of metaphysics, deconstruction, the search for a 'new language' and a 'new thinking'; philosophy as the history of philosophy or as historical knowledge; philosophy as political movementism, postmodernism, there are no facts, only interpretations; philosophy of Goofy, Pluto and Donald Duck (popsophia). One of the most obvious symptoms of this discomfort was the fact that Heidegger even had to develop an alternative theory of truth as un-concealment, i.e. a truth for philosophers that only applies to them as philosophers, while it does not apply to all other people (nor to them, unless they are philosophising).

Analytic philosophy has also participated in this strategy of residualisation. The philosopher is one who knows how to argue well, unlike the Sophists (who argue badly) and scientists (who have no need to argue because they possess the knowledge of reality). But it little matters *on what grounds* one argues. I am putting it very crudely, of course, but my aim is to explain that postmodern antirealism is just the tip of the iceberg. If this is the case, insisting on realism does not mean insisting on something unimportant or obvious. It means to say that something is unnecessarily self-limiting in the behaviour of contemporary philosophy.

Populism

It was first of all politics that undermined the postmodern hopes of emancipation.[11] The advent of media populism provided the example of a farewell to reality that was not at all emancipatory, not to mention the unscrupulous use of truth as an ideological construction, which got to the point of starting a war on the basis of false evidence of weapons of mass destruction. In the media and in several political programmes we have seen the real outcome of Nietzsche's principle that 'There are no facts, only interpretations', which only a few years earlier philosophers proposed as the way to emancipation, but which in fact presented itself as the justification for saying and doing whatever one wanted. Thus the true meaning of Nietzsche's motto turned out to be rather: 'The reason of the strongest is always the best.' This circumstance explains the slight gap in time between the end of antirealism in the analytic world[12] and the end of antirealism in the continental world. During the 1970s and 1980s, there was still much analytic antirealism and continental antirealism was still present in the departments of comparative literature.

Yet the new century showed that reality had not disappeared at all. Rather, the new media showed an augmented reality, that is, an exponential growth of recordings, fixations, inscriptions, documents that are anything but virtual – indeed, they are often all too real, as when the phone records blow up the alibi of someone accused of a crime. Take one of the oldest and most successful applications, 'AroundMe', which allows you to locate a nearby gas station, a restaurant, a pharmacy and so forth. Here we witness something very different from what is often said by the rhetoric according to which computers make us enter a second, fully virtual, life. On the contrary, we are more than ever in *this* life, the only one we have, and we perceive all too well the effect of this augmented reality, enriched with information, because at this point one could say that even the stones speak. After all, it is no coincidence that the short virtual dream of Second Life has been overtaken by the very real and often self-accusatory omnipresence on Facebook, full of documents that go as far as the description of what one has just eaten.

But even beyond such applications, the simple act of recording leads to an incalculable increase of the reality we know (i.e. what I would call 'epistemological reality', as I shall clarify later). It is fundamentally inconceivable today to have an experience like the one described by Baudelaire in *À une passante*: a fleeting beauty that disappears perhaps never to reappear again – an experience that reminds us of Poe's 'nevermore', which is in some way the essence of modernity as novelty and transience. Today Baudelaire could photograph the passer-by with his mobile phone and then begin to chase after her with a friend request on Facebook. It is obvious that rather than novelty, fleetingness and transience these conditions favour repetition, retention and rewriting. But in general, as we have said (apart from private affairs), the fact that every act is recorded significantly increases reality.

We are now aware of something that a few years ago still eluded us, despite the fact that we were already surrounded by computers: we are immersed in an archive – and we can truly realise this now, for example if we surf YouTube. What emerged with the new media is total recording. All transactions, and particularly all of our researches on the Internet, are recorded by large supranational entities, exercising a much more widespread control: it is the controlled ones that voluntarily provide information about themselves on social networks. This circumstance suggests another consideration. At a time when everything is recorded, the only protection that can be offered is via a technical difficulty (much more than by legal difficulties, since the laws are always easily circumvented by hackers).[13]

Foukant (Foucault + Kant)

Postmodern realitism is a politically motivated antirealism. Postmodernism has cultivated the idea that reality is actually constructed by power for purposes of domination, and that knowledge is not a means for emancipation, but an instrument of power. I shall name the philosophical mindset lying at the basis of this attitude 'Foukant': this fictional thinker believes (like Kant) that we do not have direct access to knowledge and that the I think must necessarily accompany our representations, and (like Foucault, in the first phase of his thought) he deems that the I think and our conceptual schemes are means for the affirmation of the will to power. Foukant's thesis ultimately consists in the following syllogism: reality is constructed by knowledge, knowledge is constructed by power, and ergo reality is constructed by power. Thus, in radical postmodernism, a logical step is taken so that reality turns out to be a construction of power, which makes it both detestable (if by 'power' we mean the Power that dominates us) and malleable (if by 'power' we mean 'in our power').

This syllogism is articulated in three fallacies. The first is the *fallacy of being-knowledge*, that is, the confusion between ontology and epistemology: between what there is and what we know about what there is. It is clear that in order to *know* that water is H_2O I need language, schemes and categories. But the fact that water *is* H_2O is utterly independent from any knowledge of mine – so much so that water was H_2O even before the birth of chemistry, and would still be if we all disappeared from the

Earth. Mostly, as regards non-scientific experience, water wets and fire burns whether I know it or not, independently from languages, schemes and categories. Something in reality resists us. It is what I call 'unamendability': the salient character of the real is that it cannot be amended or corrected at will. Which can certainly be a limitation but, at the same time, allows us to distinguish dreams from reality and science from magic.

The second is the *fallacy of ascertainment-acceptance,* on the basis of which postmodernists assumed that ascertaining reality consists in accepting the existing state of affairs and that, inversely (although with a logical gap), antirealism is emancipatory per se. Yet it is clearly not so. Antirealism is at one with acquiescence. The realist, instead, has the possibility to criticise (if they want to) and transform (if they can) by the virtue of the same banal reason why the diagnosis is the premise of therapy.

The third and essential fallacy – confirming Habermas' view that, thirty years ago, regarded postmodernism as an anti-Enlightenment groundswell,[14] – is the *fallacy of knowledge-power*, according to which behind any form of knowledge there hides a power experienced as negative. As a consequence, instead of linking itself to emancipation, knowledge becomes an instrument of enslavement. It has been rightly observed that this attitude betrays a singular 'fear of knowledge',[15] but we must not forget that together with fear there is the conviction – succinctly expressed by Cypher in *The Matrix* – that 'ignorance is bliss'. And so, with a dialectic of Enlightenment charged with consequences, the critique of knowledge turns into an escape from knowledge itself.

Deskant (Descartes + Kant)

The major premise of Foukant's syllogism ('Reality is constructed by knowledge') finds a powerful theoretical justification in constructivism, which, as I said, represents the mainstream of modern philosophy.[16] Such a perspective argues that our conceptual schemes and perceptual apparatuses play a role in the constitution of reality. I shall dub 'Deskant' the fictional philosopher embodying this view, as it begins with Descartes and culminates in Kant; it was then radicalised in the nihilistic sense by Nietzsche, or specialised in the epistemological, hermeneutic, psychological sense. This position is rooted in what I define the *transcendental fallacy*,[17] which consists in the already mentioned confusion between ontology and epistemology. At its origin there is a strategy that can be found in Descartes,[18] Hume,[19] Kant,[20] and Hegel:[21] knowledge is first of all sensible knowledge, but the senses deceive, therefore we must switch to conceptual knowledge. Constructivism is thus born out of the need to re-found, through construction, a world that no longer has stability and that, as Hamlet put it, 'is out of joint'.[22]

Now, if all knowledge begins with experience, but the latter (as empiricists suggest) is structurally uncertain, then it will be necessary to found experience through science, finding a priori structures to stabilise its uncertainty. To achieve this, we need a change of perspective: we have to start from the subjects rather than the objects, and ask ourselves – in accordance with the matrix of all subsequent constructionism – not how things are in themselves, but how they should be made in order to be known by us, following the model of physicists who question nature not as scholars, but as judges: that is, using schemes and theorems.

Deskant then adopts an a priori epistemology, i.e. mathematics, to found ontology: the possibility of synthetic a priori judgements allows us to fixate an otherwise fluid reality through certain knowledge. In this way, transcendental philosophy moved constructionism from the sphere of mathematics to that of ontology.[23] The laws of physics and mathematics are applied to reality and, in Deskant's hypothesis, they are not the contrivance of a group of scientists, but they are the way in which our minds and senses work. Our knowledge, at this point, will no longer be threatened by the unreliability of the senses and the uncertainty of induction, but the price we have to pay is that there is no longer any difference between the fact that *there is* an object X and the fact that we *know* the object X. Of course, Kant invites us to think that behind the phenomenal object X there is a noumenal object Y, a thing-in-itself inaccessible to us, but the fact remains that the sphere of being coincides to a very large extent with that of the knowable, and that the knowable is essentially equivalent to the constructible.[24]

At the origin of the transcendental fallacy there is therefore an interweaving of topics:

1 the senses deceive (they are not 100 per cent certain);
2 induction is uncertain (it is not 100 per cent certain);
3 science is safer than experience, because it has mathematical principles independent from the deceptions of the senses and the uncertainties of induction;

4 experience must then be resolved in science (it must be founded by science or, at worst, it must be unmasked by it as a misleading 'manifest image');

5 since science is the construction of paradigms, at this point experience will be construction too, namely it will shape the world starting from conceptual schemes.

Here is the origin of postmodernism.

Upon closer inspection, at the heart of the whole matter we find the concept of causality. Descartes's problem is to explain how the world can affect the cogito if the cogito is not part of the world. Kant's problem is instead to explain how the world can produce effects on the transcendental subject if causality is a category that belongs to the transcendental subject himself. By placing causality between his transcendental categories, Kant condemns himself to an implicitly idealist form of constructivism, because it prevents the world from exercising a genuine causal effect on the subject.[25] This is the crux of Deskant's thesis: the world has no causal power on the subject both because the subject is not part of the world (Descartes) and because causality belongs solely to the subject (Kant).

It is worth noting that Kant, unlike Deskant and Foukant, had already become aware of this difficulty with the *Critique of Judgement*, through which he rejected the *Critique of Pure Reason*. First, in the critique of aesthetic judgement, Kant wrote that the beautiful is liked without a concept: in other words, he dethroned conceptuality and did so in an area where perception is particularly important. Second, in the critique of teleological judgement, Kant explicitly proposed a theory of science: nature has no end in itself, it is we who assign ends to it so as to be able to scientifically investigate it. Third, Kant argued that the reflective judgement introduced in the Third Critique, which starts from the single instance and rises to the general rule, should be set next to the determinant judgement of the First Critique, which descends from the general rule to the single instance; nevertheless, there are good reasons to believe that what he referred to was the need to replace the determinant judgement rather than merely integrating it. In fact, it is hard to see how the determinant judgement could co-exist with the reflective judgement, in a strange amphibious mode where it would be up to the subject to choose which to employ. In any case, even if the subject resorted to the reflective judgement (and we can be sure that they would only use that one), they would not be able to reply to the objections brought forward by Hume, because in fact the reflective judgement is in all respects the empiricist induction, which starts from the single instance and rises to the rule.

T-Rex

The function that I shall oppose to Foukant and Deskant, T-Rex, is not a human being, but an animal – more precisely, a dinosaur. Dinosaurs lived between the Upper Triassic (about 230 million years ago) and the end of the Cretaceous (about 65 million years ago). The first human beings and their conceptual schemes appeared 250,000 years ago according to some and 500,000 years ago according to others. For 165 million years there were dinosaurs but no humans. For 64 million years there have been neither humans nor dinosaurs. For half a million years now there have been humans but no dinosaurs.

This circumstance, which I call 'argument of pre-existence',[26] constitutes a problem for Deskant. For him, thought is the first and immediate object we experience and we have no contact with the world 'out there', if not through the mediation of thought and its categories.[27] According to Deskant, natural objects are located in space and time, which, however, only exist in our minds, together with the categories we use to understand the world. One would have to conclude that before people existed there were no objects, or at least not as we know them, but clearly it is not the case. T-Rex existed before Foukant or Deskant and before any 'I think' in general. How can we deal with this?

A good move could be that of trying to understand how, according to constructivists, the linguistic–conceptual dimension constitutes the real. There are two possible cases: either reality is actually constructed by our concepts, and then dinosaurs have never existed (at most there are their fossils, that magically appeared at the precise moment when a human being discovered them); or reality is not made up of concepts, but of objects – like the dinosaurs that lived before humans – and conceptual schemes are only useful for relating to what remains of dinosaurs, so as to try and understand how they looked like and how they lived, i.e. so as to fulfil an *epistemological* function and not an ontological one.

Now let's look at the possible kinds of the world's dependence on conceptual schemes, from the strongest to the weakest. Consider the strongest dependence, namely that brought forward by those who assert (in the form of an extreme correlationalism) that being only exists as a correlate of thought. In this case, one could hypothesise that being causally depends on thought: the dinosaur depends on the I think. In this strong version, the dependence of the objects on thought is, then, an explicit causal dependence. The subjects 'somehow' cause the objects, if only because they are their necessary epistemological condition. Without knowing subjects, there are no known objects,[28] and this is beyond dispute. But (and here is the point missed by the proponent of causal dependence) it does not mean that without subjects there would be no objects at all. The origin of this lies in a famous argument of Berkeley's, which is epistemological and not ontological: if a tree falls in a forest and no one is around to hear it, it makes no noise. But since, in this version, being (ontology) depends on knowledge (epistemology), the supporter of causal dependence concludes that the tree has not really fallen until someone certifies its fall. From which it obviously follows that dinosaurs never existed, since when they were around (assuming that an expression of this kind, at this point, has any meaning at all) we were not there.

In order to avoid the misinterpretations of causal dependence, antirealists sometimes speak of conceptual dependence, which is one of the possible outcomes of Kant's famous statement: 'intuitions without concepts are blind'. However, this sentence can be interpreted in two ways: (1) without the concept of 'dinosaur' we would not recognise a dinosaur if we saw one; and (2) without the concept of 'dinosaur' we would not *see* a dinosaur if we saw one. When it comes to defending Kant, it is said that he meant (1): the conceptual is reconstructive of experience in general. But had he meant (1), he would not have written the *Critique of Pure Reason*, but only the *Metaphysical Foundations Of Natural Science*,[29] namely a theory of science. If he wrote the *Critique of Pure Reason*, it is because he meant (2): concepts are constitutive of experience in general. So much so that in the chapter on schematism he even provides the scheme of the dog, without which, we must suppose, dogs would lead a noumenal existence at best.[30] Now, if causal dependence is invalidated by the pre-existence argument, conceptual dependence is invalidated by the interaction argument, which is the following. If I now met an extremely long-lived or revived dinosaur, I could interact with it even though its conceptual schemes are likely to be very different from mine. As I will develop in 'Positivity', we generally interact with beings who have conceptual schemes and perceptual apparatuses that are profoundly different from our own, or have none at all.

In order to avoid the argument of pre-existence and that of interaction, antirealists refer to 'representational dependence': we are not the creators of the universe, but we are its constructors starting from an amorphous *hyle*.[31] Here is the mainstream of modern philosophy, which – as I hope I have shown – is not nihilism or solipsism (which impacts too heavily on common sense), but constructivism, i.e. the idea that reality is there, but is amorphous in itself, a dough for cookies, an undifferentiated *chora* which is modelled by the subjects, who become constructors of phenomena. In other words, the world and the things in themselves that we encounter inside it are granted existence, but not independence. This then makes it possible to assert with confidence that the existence of things was never denied, adding that we have access only to phenomena and never to things in themselves, so that regarding something as a thing-in-itself is an inexcusable naivety in a person minimally cultivated in terms of philosophy.

Thus the separate existence of a world is acknowledged, but the world as such is taken to have no structural and morphological autonomy, at least not that we know of. The thing-in-itself could potentially be the Matrix. Yet, representational dependence turns out not to work either. In fact, there are two options. Either the *word* 'Tyrannosaurus Rex' depends on us, and then there is no serious dependence. Or, just like with causal dependence (which is the only serious kind of dependence) the *being* of the Tyrannosaurus Rex depends on humans, which does not work given that when the Tyrannosaurus Rex existed we did not – it would paradoxically follow that when there were dinosaurs, dinosaurs were not there.[32] At this point, perhaps an antirealist might object: how can you prove the existence of a dinosaur independently of thought? But the answer would be simple: 'It is you that must provide a proof. You are here to prove dinosaurs' dependence on thought, which is what, so far, you have not done.'

Part Two

Positivity

Let us now turn to positivity, that is, the metaphysical core of new realism. As I said, if the realist is the one who claims that there are parts of the world that are not dependent on the subjects, the new realist asserts something more challenging. Not only are there large parts of the world independent of the *cogito*, but those parts are inherently structured, and thus orientate the behaviour and thought of humans as well as animals.

Unamendability

Making perceptual experience (and not, as we shall see, social reality) depend on conceptual schemes requires at least two steps. The first is, so to speak, a sort of phenomenological carelessness. You would have to be very gullible indeed to mistake a greenish afterimage for a patch on the wall; of course it can happen, but it usually never does. Therefore, the first move made by new realism is an empirical observation. The grain of what is perceived is much finer than that of what is merely thought, recalled or represented. You can look at a remembered sun without hurting your eyes; a remembered duck-rabbit does not shift; comparing two remembered colours is always problematic because the real shades have a finer grain than the memory of them. If this is how things are, then the problem consisted merely of assimilating, under the name 'representation', things that are in fact very diverse, only to draw the conclusion that the control of representations derives from conceptual schemes, in line with the constructionism brought forward by Deskant and Foukant.

The second element is what psychologists call the 'stimulus error', by which they mean the ease with which we replace an observation with an explanation. In other words, it is the ease with which, when we have our eyes closed, we reply 'nothing' or 'blackness' to the question 'what do you see?', when what we see are really phosphines and flashes. We do not include those in our description because we are talking about something else, namely a theory of vision for which the eye is like a *camera obscura*,[1] so that when the shutter is closed there is total darkness. When one argues that observers equipped with different theories see reality differently,[2] one gives philosophical dignity to a psychological error, and most importantly makes a category mistake that lies in confusing seeing with knowing. For example, if I read the word 'rapresentational dependence' (sic) *I think* of 'representational dependence', but I see 'rapresentational dependence' (sic).

Now, there is a class of representations that the I think will never be able to accompany: that of the infinite number of things that existed before any I think. I have already called this 'argument of pre-existence': the world is given prior to any cogito. Then there are classes of representations that, even though accompanied by the I think, seem to resist it, regardless of the 'representational dependence'; I call this 'argument of resistance':[3] reality may oppose refusals to our conceptual schemes. I collect these empirical circumstances – which, however, have a transcendental role, since they define, even though in retrospect, our possibilities of knowledge – under the name of unamendability:[4] the key feature of what there is lies in its prevalence over epistemology, because it cannot be corrected – and this is, after all, an infinitely more powerful necessity than any logical necessity.[5]

The unamendability of the real determines the non-conceptual content of experience.[6] It is a contrastive principle, which manifests the real as non-I. The inherently deconstructive role of perception, ultimately, is this: rather than a source of information and an epistemological resource, it should be considered a stumbling block to set against our constructivist expectations. In a way, perceptual deconstruction is comparable to falsification in Popper,[7] except that here it has an ontological function and not an epistemological one. Here we find the importance of perception as well as the ontological meaning of aesthetics as *aisthesis*:[8] the senses sometimes disprove our theories. The basic argument does not consist in saying that the stick immersed in water appears broken because it really is broken, but in pointing out that, although we know that the stick immersed in water is not broken, we can do nothing *but* see it broken.[9]

In my opinion, this is the decisive reason for the philosophical importance of sensibility: its does not passively confirm our expectations and knowledge. On the contrary, it often opposes them, clearly revealing that there is something distinct and separate from us. What emerges is a 'naive physics'[10] or a 'second naiveté':[11] the world presents itself to us as real without necessarily claiming on that account to be scientifically true.[12] As I understand it, the appeal to simplicity is not a way to simplify, but to sophisticate, our relationship with reality. This is where one draws the dialectic that leads from unamendability to affirmativity.

Ontology

In its resistance, the real is the negative of knowledge, because it is the inexplicable and the incorrigible; but it is also the positive of being, because it is what is given, resisting interpretation, and distinguishing itself from fantasy or wishful thinking. We must not forget that in areas dependent on conceptual schemes, such as historical events, we can find a clear manifestation of unamendability, namely the irrevocable character of the past events on which the interpretations of historians are constructed. Now, interpretations take place on the basis of facts and facts occur in a world of objects. If this is the case, then the acknowledgement of facts in the physical world (for example, the fact that snow is white) is placed at a perfectly continuous level with respect to the acknowledgement of facts in the historical world. The negativity of the unamendable thus signals the positivity of ontology.

The second move of new realism is conceptual clarification,[13] which focuses (against the fallacy of being-knowledge and against the transcendental fallacy) on stressing the difference between ontology (that is independent of our representations) and epistemology (that *may* be dependent on our representations, keeping in mind that what makes our statements true are not our representations, but that to which those representations relate). Now, it makes perfect sense to assume that there is a conceptual action taking place when I recognise a constellation,[14] or when, looking at three objects, I believe – like Leśniewski – that for every two objects there is one that is their sum, multiplying their number.[15] But this conflict can be explained by the simple consideration that we cannot see properly neither the constellations nor Leśniewski's objects, but only the stars and the three objects of common sense.

This is not to argue that constellations are not real, but rather to draw a difference (which obviously stems from the difference between ontology and epistemology) between two layers of reality that fade into each other. The first is what I would call *ε-reality*, meaning by this 'epistemological reality', or what the Germans call 'Realität'. It is the reality linked to what (we think) we know about what there is, which is why I call it 'epistemological'. This is the reality referred to by Kant when he says that 'intuitions without concepts are blind'; or by Quine when he says that 'to be is to be the value of a variable.'[16] But next to, or rather below, the ε-reality I also set the *ω-reality* in the sense of ὄντως (I use the omega just to make a distinction): that is, the ontological reality, or what the Germans call 'Wirklichkeit', which refers to what there is whether we know it or not, and which manifests itself both as a resistance (unamendability) and as positivity.[17]

Ω-reality is the external world – expression by which, as can be seen from the following scheme, I mean the world external to conceptual schemes. At this point it is time to introduce, along with the difference between ontology and epistemology, that between ontological independence and epistemological independence. The way in which the problem of realism has been set in the analytic area defines realism as independence of *truth* from the knowledge we have of it. For new realism,[18] instead, it is independence of *reality* from the knowledge we have of it (while maintaining that, in certain classes of objects, this may not be the case). I believe this aspect is important because truth is, in any case, an epistemological function, which presupposes minds: a sentence like 'On 17 September, 1873 Bismarck had a flu' is causally independent of minds, but it presupposes them. And so (we will get back to this) the formula of the independence of truth from human minds lends itself well to some aspects of social reality. Thus, new realism proposes its distinctions, which can be summed up as follows.[19]

Epistemology Amendable	**Ontology** Unamendable
Science Linguistic Historical Free Infinite Teleological	**Experience** Not necessarily linguistic Not historical Necessary Finite Not necessarily teleological

Truth Not born out of experience, but teleologically oriented towards it	**Reality** Not naturally oriented towards science
Internal world (= internal to conceptual schemes)	**External world** (= external to conceptual schemes)

I believe that the distinction between ontology and epistemology (as well as the distinctions that follow, between external world and internal world, and between science and experience) responds to two essential realist needs so as to overcome the fallacy of being-knowledge, which started with transcendental philosophy and culminated in postmodernism. On the one hand, we should maintain that there is an unamendable kernel in being and experience that gives itself in complete independence from conceptual schemes and knowledge. On the other hand, we must leave open the possibility of constructing, starting from this unamendable layer, knowledge as a conceptual, linguistic, deliberate, and especially emancipatory activity.

Interaction

Let us now come to the third move, granted by the stability of the ontological ground: the acknowledgement of interaction. Reality has a structured nature that precedes conceptual schemes and can resist them. So there is no need to rely on an a priori epistemology to stabilise contingency. One of our most common experiences is that we interact with beings who have conceptual schemes and perceptual apparatuses different from our own (or that do not have such things at all), such as dogs, cats, flies and so forth. Well, if interaction depended on conceptual schemes and knowledge, it would be somehow miraculous. Unless we wish to resort to the hypothesis of a miracle or a pre-established harmony, we are forced to admit that interaction is made possible by the sharing of a common and homogeneous space, and of objects independent of our conceptual schemes.

The fact that negativity turns into positivity and resistance into possibility is thus not a conceptual alchemy but a piece of evidence that comes to us precisely from interaction.[20] In short, the point is not to know what it feels like to be a bat, but rather to note the fact that humans and bats unquestionably inhabit the same world.[21] Both a man and a cat know how to use the seat of a chair (the former to sit down, the latter to curl up on it) and can fight over it: this does not seem to depend on the sharing of concepts, but on the positivity of the specific object, that is, the seat of a chair.

If we look back at Kant's thought, we will note that it is anthropocentric and his revolution is Ptolemaic, not Copernican, because it places the human subject at the centre of the universe. Now, what has to be made clear is that epistemology, as a human construct, is anthropocentric, but ontology is not, as it manifests itself first of all as resistance. And even when it presents itself as affordance it is not only addressed to humans. In accordance with other thinkers,[22] I propose that we abandon Kant's Ptolemaic revolution and reach the end of anthropocentrism in ontology. Of course, in epistemology you can do whatever you want. But the important thing is not to make anthropocentric mistakes in ontology.

The idea that the world constitutes a positivity regardless of our thought, our conceptual schemes and so on is well explained through what I have defined as the slipper experiment.[23] It simply points out that beings so different as a man, a dog, a worm, a plant, or even a slipper can interact with one another regardless of their sharing of representations or schemes. Of course, I never thought that a dog, a constructivist and myself all see the world the same way. I am saying that we can interact *despite* the fact that our conceptual schemes and perceptual apparatuses are different, and that this interaction is possible because it takes place in a shared world (it is much easier to explain it in this way than by resorting to a divine intervention).

The point, though, is that it is far from obvious that when we turn to the world instead of thought we should fall into uncertainty. As usual, Deskant is too sceptical of objects, their solidity, their positivity. With the transcendental fallacy Kant tried to reply to Hume, who had insisted on the contingency of the laws of nature and the structural uncertainty of induction. Kant's answer consisted in founding experience by means of science, and science through a system of a priori categories that, according to him, drew their necessary character from their very apriority. Now – and this is the great metaphysical intuition proposed by Kripke,[24] the consequences of which have probably not been fully exploited yet – necessity does not derive from apriority, and there may be a posteriori principles that are necessary. Thus, there is *de re* necessity or, as I would call it, ontological necessity, which has to be distinguished from epistemological necessity (which is *de dicto*, and is derived and not foundational of ontological necessity). After all, Aristotle, whom Kant rebuked for picking up his categories in a 'rhapsodic' way, gave birth to a much more solid construct than the Kantian one – in fact, 'place', 'time' and 'situation' survived the passing of time much better than the category of 'reciprocal action'. If this is the case, the need underlying the transcendental fallacy is revealed as a mere misunderstanding that arises precisely from having identified necessity with apriority and aposteriority (i.e. the object) with contingency.

Affordance

Let us now come to the fourth move made by new realism, which consists in regarding affordance as the other side of unamendability. Interaction shows that reality does not only manifest itself as resistance and negativity: every negation entails a determination and a possibility. The world exerts an affordance,[25] through the objects and the environment, which qualifies as a positive realism. The first essential principle of positive realism is therefore that the world does not merely say no: it does not only resist us. It is also the greatest ontological positivity. In order to illustrate this point I would like to consider the debate that took place roughly twenty years ago between a constructivist, Richard Rorty, and a negative realist, Umberto Eco.[26] With the aim of demonstrating the world's plasticity with regards to our vital objectives, Rorty affirmed that a screwdriver is not to be merely used with screws: one can also scratch one's ear with it, for instance. Eco replied that it is indeed possible, adding that one could use it as a weapon as well (Eco referred to the 'screwdriver murders' on Italian streets in the 1960s). Yet this does not mean that you could do *anything* with a screwdriver: you cannot clean your ears with it, because it is too long and sharp. It is as simple as that: the constructionist claims that reality is docile in respect of our purposes, while the negative realist objects that it can also say 'no' to us.

In this regard it is necessary to clarify a statement that might seem too trenchant. Facts have the characteristic of being independent of us and of affecting us (i.e. of acting causally on us), and this is their fundamental value. However, 'value' is usually a standard against which to assess things and facts. Beauty is a value in the sense that it allows us to evaluate something as more/less beautiful, and similarly justice allows us to evaluate something as more/less just. Instead, facts are not 'more/less real' but simply real, and they do not allow us to evaluate anything other than themselves. Another way to express this difference is to say that facts exist exerting causality while values exist exerting normativity. However, as will be clear in the part of this essay dedicated to emergence, normativity derives from the sphere of facts, so causality is the necessary (though not sufficient) condition of normativity.

Now, one should not underestimate the power of those facts we call 'objects'. Children in a pre-linguistic age are already able to segment linguistic reality into objects – which for Deskant, strictly speaking, would not be possible, given that, presumably, children do not possess the scheme of substance as permanence in time. The thesis I defend through the argument of affordance is that we should start from the objects (an area in which subjects are also included), so as to reduce the gap between our theories and our experience of the world. This is not meant to be a futile worship of objectivity (which is a property of knowledge, not of being), but a due recognition of the positivity on which we all rely, but upon which we rarely reflect. And this does not only apply to physical experiences: the way in which beauty, or moral value or non-value come forward clearly shows that there is something outside us, surprising and striking us. And this something has value precisely *because* it comes from outside: otherwise it would be nothing but imagination. That is why, contrary to what is often said, one cannot distinguish the value from the fact: this is because the fact is itself a value, and the highest one, i.e. positivity, which in turn is the condition of possibility of each value.

We can better understand this by means of the experiment of the ethical brain, which is a variation of the *Gedankenexperiment* of the brain in a vat.[27] The idea is this: imagine that a mad scientist has put some brains in a vat and is feeding them artificially. By means of electrical stimulation, these brains have the impression of living in a real world, but in fact what they feel is the result of simple electrical stimulations. Imagine that those stimulations depict situations that require moral stances: some snitch and some sacrifice themselves for freedom, some commit embezzlement and some commit acts of holiness. Can we really say that in those circumstances there are moral acts taking place? In my opinion, we cannot: these are, in the best-case scenario, representations with moral content. To put it a little peremptorily, without the positivity of objects no morality is possible.

Objects

At this point – and this is the fifth move made by new realism – it becomes possible to articulate the characteristics of the affordance that comes to us from the objects. We need to begin by introducing the categories of natural objects (such as tables and chairs, which exist in space and time independently of the subjects) and ideal objects (such as numbers or theorems, which exist outside of space and in time, independently of the subject). Then we must add two new categories: that of artefacts (such as mobile phones and computers), which exist in space and time depending on the subjects for their genesis, and that of social objects (such as weddings and funerals), which exist in space and time depending on the subjects for their genesis *and* their persistence. From this point of view, it is entirely legitimate to assert that the stock market or democracy are representationally dependent on our collective beliefs. But this does not mean in any way that dinosaurs have some degree of dependence with respect to our collective beliefs. If anything, dependence concerns professorships in paleontology.

In particular, the distinction between natural objects and social objects seems to be decisive to circumvent the fallacy of ascertainment-acceptance, and to make social reality into a concrete ground of analysis and transformation. On the one hand, in fact, it allows us to recognise the natural world as independent of human construction, avoiding the nihilistic and sceptical outcome that is reached when trying to dialecticise the distinction between nature and culture. On the other hand, it allows us to see the social world as the work of human construction, which however – precisely to the extent to which it is social – is not a purely subjective production. In this way, the sphere of natural objects, as well as that of social objects, becomes the field of a possible and legitimate knowledge, i.e. of epistemology – which undoubtedly involves hermeneutics, since in many cases knowledge requires varying degrees of interpretation.

Nevertheless, this epistemology has a very different value depending on whether it refers to natural objects or social objects. In respect of the former, in fact, epistemology exerts a purely reconstructive function, merely acknowledging something that exists independently of knowledge itself (for instance, the fact that water is H_2O or that Rameses II died of tuberculosis). In respect of social objects, however, epistemology has a constitutive value, both in the sense that a certain amount of knowledge is necessary to live in any social world, and in the sense that in the social world new objects are produced (for example, through the legislative activity) with an operation that is not purely one of acknowledgement (as is the reference to natural objects), but is performative.

In this sense I claim, with a form of contextualism, that one is never fully realist or antirealist. There are spheres of being that can be more or less close to the focal meaning of existence as resistance in an environment. Hence, instead of realism one should speak of 'realisms'. In fact, saying that everything is socially constructed and that there are no facts, only interpretations, means not deconstructing but, on the contrary, formulating a thesis – the more accommodating in reality the more critical it is in imagination – that leaves everything as it is. There is indeed a great conceptual work that interpretation-friendly thinkers withdraw from when they say that everything is socially constructed – which, *nota bene*, implies that tables and chairs do not have a separate existence: that is, to put it more bluntly, that they do not really exist in the mode of existence that common sense usually attributes to tables and chairs. This work consists in distinguishing carefully between the existence of things that exist only for us, i.e. things that only exist if there is a mankind, and things that would exist even if humans had never been there. That is why, in my opinion, the real deconstruction must commit to distinguishing between regions of being that are socially constructed and others that are not; to establishing for each region of being some specific modes of existence, and finally to ascribing individual objects to one of these regions of being, proceeding case by case.

In this regard it is necessary to make one last consideration about hermeneutics, which postmodernism rather weirdly claimed the monopoly of. When I oppose the statement that 'there are no facts, only interpretations' I do not at all mean to argue that there are no interpretations – there surely are, especially in the social world. But the first and fundamental interpretation consists in discerning between what can be interpreted and what cannot be interpreted, what links exist between ontology and epistemology and what is the relevance of the latter with regard to natural, social and ideal objects. In the social world, epistemology undoubtedly matters to a great extent because it is constitutive with respect to ontology (whereas, in the natural world, it is only reconstructive: it finds something that exists independently of epistemology); what we think, what we say, our interactions are all crucial, and it is crucial that these interactions are recorded and documented. This is why the social world is full of documents: in archives, in our drawers, in our wallets, and now even on our mobile phones.

It is in this context that hermeneutics can play an important role, all the more important because – as I have said earlier – there is a clear distinction between natural objects, ideal objects and social objects. The first task of hermeneutics is to distinguish between these types of objects. That is the first and most important of all interpretations, which hermeneutics has often rejected by limiting itself to obvious statements ('there are interpretations and not just facts') or false ones ('there are no facts, only interpretations').

In this perspective, I propose the spheres of being are reconstructed as things in themselves and not as phenomena. I shall leave ideal objects aside and focus on the other two kinds. Let us begin with natural objects. As we have seen, for Deskant they are the phenomena *par excellence*: they are situated in space and time, and yet they are not to be found in nature. They are in our minds, along with the categories we use to give order to the world, to the point that, without human beings, space and time – as well as the objects they contain – may disappear. As I have shown, however, Deskant was wrong: natural objects are, indeed, things in themselves.

Upon closer inspection, it becomes clear that social objects are also things in themselves and not phenomena. This may seem complicated at first because, if social objects depend on conceptual schemes, then it should obviously follow that they are phenomena. But it is not so. In order to be a phenomenon, it is not enough to depend on conceptual schemes. A phenomenon must also be opposed to the thing-in-itself. Let us consider a fine. What would be its 'in-itself'? To say that a fine is an apparent fine is to simply say that it is not a fine; a true fine is a thing-in-itself. Above all, people are things in themselves, while in Deskant's view they would turn into ghosts or shadowy projections of thought. And now let us come to events, things like hurricanes or car accidents, which are often unpredictable. Irregularity, i.e. what disregards our data and expectations, is the clearest demonstration of the fact that the world is much more extensive and unpredictable than our thinking, and that there are many more things in themselves than Deskant was willing to admit.

Environment

The sixth and final move of new realism consists in isolating the concept of environment. Everything, including corporations, symbolist poems and categorical imperatives, has its origin in the affordance offered by the environment. A cave has affordances for different types of beings and serves as a shelter because it has certain characteristics and not others. But think of infinitely more complex structures such as eco systems, state organisations, interpersonal relationships: in each of these we find the same structure of resistance and affordance, which from causality may (though not necessarily) evolve into normativity. I define 'environment' as every sphere in which these interactions take place, from an ecological niche to the social world – of course, each with its own characteristics.

It is in this regard that I believe we should set against Markus Gabriel's thesis 'to exist is to exist in a field of sense' the thesis 'to exist is to exist in an environment'. The former means that, for instance, Harry Potter exists in the field of meaning of fantastic literature and atoms exist in that of physics. The only thing that, for Gabriel, does not exist is the world, understood not as the physical universe, but as the sum of all fields of sense: the field of sense of all fields of sense (i.e. the absolute) does not exist. Nevertheless, making ontology depend on a field of sense – that is, if not on epistemology at least on something tied to subjectivity – re-proposes a version of the transcendental fallacy, though a weakened one. Furthermore, it leaves open the problem of non-human beings, i.e. those we call (in such a confused manner) 'animals': it is hard to claim that there is, for them, a field of sense in which there are atoms or characters like Harry Potter. But it is problematic (also from a moral point of view) to exclude the existence, for instance, of death in a slaughterhouse – which, nonetheless, can be hardly inserted (both for an animal and for a human) into a 'field of sense', since it presents itself as an opaque and resisting nonsense.

This is the condition I propose we call 'ontological opacity', namely the antithesis of the equation between rationality and reality. There is no logical answer to the question 'why something rather than nothing?', just as we have no difficulty in thinking that ideal objects has always existed, even before the Big Bang. This does not mean that the rational is unreal, nor (even less!) that the real is irrational. It means that epistemology is an outcome of thought, which is in turn the result of an evolutionary story which began in something that is being and not thought.

Now, an event or an object – from the Holocaust to Kafka's Odradek – can seem to be utterly senseless, but this does not mean that the event did not take place or that the object does not exist. The fact that we sometimes find ourselves unable to find any meaning in our lives does not mean that we do not exist. The perspective suggested by 'to exist is to exist in an environment', instead, is that of a structurally opaque existence that manifests itself first of all in its persistence and possibly in its acting in an environment, without further qualifications. In other words, the field of sense is in the environment and not in the head; it is in the affordance and not in the concepts. Obviously, starting from the objects and from the opacity of existence involves being aware that ontology and epistemology are not sharply distinguished, but that our relationship with the world is rather the outcome of a confusing balance between ontology and epistemology. This, however, does not mean that the positivity of objects is precluded to us. Indeed, it is this very positivity that allows us to dwell in the world despite the fact that our notions are rarely clear and distinct.

Affordances have an epistemologically important consequence. Eugene Wigner, Nobel Prize-winner for physics, has spoken of 'the unreasonable effectiveness of mathematics'; along the same lines, Hilary Putnam has enunciated the miracle argument: if there was no *one* reality working as a substratum both for the world of life and that of science, how would we explain the fact that the latter is so efficacious on the first? Through a sort of occasionalism? By means of a pre-established harmony? The problem with this argument of Putnam's is, though, that it exposes itself to a counter-objection, because the antirealist could reply: 'If you cannot give me valid arguments in favour of realism apart from the functional efficaciousness of science, then this efficaciousness might very well be simply a miracle, and yours an act of faith.'

Now, it is in this environment that the emergence of thought from being occurs; such a process can be regarded as the development of an (intelligent) epistemology on the basis of an unintelligent ontology, a competence that precedes comprehension. The fact that the meaning is not in the head, but in the world, is a principle well illustrated in the social world and its media, which I regard as equivalent and locate in the sphere of documentality. But even outside of the social sphere, being is not something constructed by thought, it is given before thought comes to be. Not only because we know of interminable periods in which there was the world, but there were no people, but also because what initially appears as thought actually comes from outside of us: the words of our mother, the myths and rules, the totems and taboos that we encounter in everyday life are merely *found* by us, just as in Mecca one comes across a meteorite.

We encounter objects that have an ontological consistence independently from our knowledge and that *then*, either suddenly or through a slow process, are known by us. We find out parts of ourselves (for instance, that we are envious or that we have fear of mice) just like we discover pieces of nature. We notice elements of society (for instance, enslavement, exploitation, women's subordination and then, with a greater sensitivity, also mobbing or political incorrectness) that turn out to be unbearable and were previously hidden, namely assumed as obvious by a political or social unconscious. The moment of awareness will hopefully come, but it will be a matter of detachment with respect to a previous adherence, not an act of absolute construction of the world by the means of thought. In the psychological and social world, the motto could be 'I am therefore I (sometimes) think'. And what I think is not the result of an absolute, constitutive and independent intentionality, but of a documentality made of traditions, languages and influences that draw the psychic world no less than the social.

Hence the thesis of the dependence (of which I have already spoken) and, furthermore, the argument of the derivation of epistemology from ontology. All the essential differences that govern our thinking – and that we tend to forget, even though they guide our practices – are derived from reality, not from thought: consider the differences between ontology and epistemology, experience and science, the external world and the internal world, objects and events, facts and fiction.

So, *metaphysical realism* (if we grant that such a position ever really existed as it is represented by antirealists) supposes a full mirroring of thought and reality:

(1) Thought ↔ Reality

Constructivism, finding this relation between two distinct realities incomprehensible, suggests a constitutive role of thought with respect to reality:

(2) Thought → Reality

Positive realism, instead, sees thought as an emerging datum of reality, just like gravity, photosynthesis and digestion.[28]

(3) Thought ← Reality

Part Three

Normativity

In the final part of this book I would like to address the sphere of the social world. If what I said about the environment is true, then it is clear that the meaning is not in the head, but in the world. We are not constructors of meaning: at most, we are receptors of meaning. And if we move from the generic abstraction 'man' to the multitude of human beings, and especially to the vast number of social objects (and now also of electronic devices) that they incessantly produce, we will see how little truth lies in Vico's saying that society is transparent because it is the product of man. The surprises that many documents hold for us, the power they wield on the subject even beyond the intentions of the latter, the possibility – immanent in every form of writing – of initiating automatic processes beyond the control of those who created them are all evidence of the unpredictability of objects, even when they depend on the social world for their genesis (in the case of artefacts) and existence (in that of social objects). It is in this already-structured world that normativity originates, because that is where lies the foundation of the human being as the 'animal that promises' (as Nietzsche concisely said) or as an 'inherently normative being' (as Brandom said less concisely). It is from these assumptions that I propose my reconstruction of the social world.

Documentality[1]

Marshall McLuhan was a great thinker and a man of spirit. We owe him a fundamental motto: 'I've always been careful never to predict anything that had not already happened.' Unfortunately, however, in one case – and not a marginal one – he has not fulfilled his obligation: it is when he argued that the age of writing was over.[2] We can certainly imagine that in the middle of last century, a time full of telephones and televisions, one could actually believe that the end of writing was a fact. But then again, it is now a fact that things have gone in the diametrically opposed direction, towards a boom of writing. At one point, the keys of the typewriter appeared on the mobile phone – i.e. the absolute speaking machine – and never left.[3]

Little by little, we stopped talking and started to write, and now we write all day. When we are not writing on our phone, we read on it: in fact, mobile phones have become bigger precisely so as to make it easier for us to read and write on them. And in the rare moments when we are not reading or writing, we record (taking pictures, shooting videos, taking notes etc.): that is, we transform the 'verba volant' into 'scripta manent'. Of course, it is not without irony that the prophet of the end of writing has been remembered by Canada, on the centenary of his birth, with a postage stamp. Let's say, however, that the postmodern and Baumanian hypothesis of the so-called 'liquid modernity',[4] which defines contemporary society as characterised by great instability, is countered precisely by the fixation and stabilisation brought about by the enormous growth of records. We have never had less a liquid and more a granitic society, as is well known by all those who, after recklessly posting some inappropriate comments on a social network, see their life and career destroyed – at the court of Versailles or Constantinople there was definitely more tolerance.

The boom of writing is one of the most significant proofs of the relevance of what I call 'documentality',[5] that is, the environment in which social objects are generated. In the definition of documentality the concepts of technique, writing and recording are central. Technique is, strictly speaking, any possibility of recording, which heralds the possibility of iteration: that is, the most manifest form in which technology comes into our experience. Now, the technology of all technologies, in our historical experience, is writing. And contrary to what was posited by Plato, writing has three incalculable advantages compared to what takes place in the inner life of the soul. First, public accessibility. No one can look into the minds of others, but to read the texts of others is more than possible; contracts, money, encyclopaedias: all of the social world and the world of knowledge require recourse to the written word. Second, while internal writing is destined to disappear with us, external writing can survive even when we die. Third, there is the ability to produce more copies of the same entity (a form of repetition that it would perhaps be more appropriate to define as 'instantiation').[6]

Especially, note this: if we look at the essence, any form of recording is a kind of writing. A video or voice message that you can play as you like (which today is technically very easy) are forms of writing, just as a computer file or a written piece of paper. If we consider that recording, as permanence of the memory trace, is also the condition of possibility of thought – as suggested by the old metaphor of the mind as a *tabula*, i.e. a writing surface – it is not difficult to recognise the centrality of this category, which was instead systematically neglected in favour of others (mind, action …) in the analysis of the construction of social and mental reality.[7]

From this point of view, it is possible to assert that society is not based on communication, but on recording. Given that – as we saw at the beginning of this chapter – there is nothing social outside the text, papers, archives and documents constitute the foundation of the social world. I repeat: society is not based on communication, but on recording, which is the condition for the creation of social objects. Man is socialised through recording. Bare life is but a remote start; culture begins very early, manifesting itself through recordings and imitation (language, rituals). This explains why writing, as well as the sphere of recordings that precedes and surrounds writing, is so important.

Equipped with these tools, we now have a system that explains both the media and social reality, even in its bureaucratic dimension. The constitutive law of social objects is 'object =

recorded act'. That is to say, a social object is the result of (1) a social act (which means, an act that involves at least two people, or a machine and a person) that is (2) characterised by being recorded on a piece of paper, a computer file, or even only in the minds of the people involved. Social objects are divided into documents in the strong sense, as inscriptions of acts, and documents in the weak sense, as recordings of facts. A strong document is one that has some kind of power (such documents are, for example, banknotes, tickets, contracts), while a weak document is one that merely keeps track of what has taken place, such as, for example, expired tickets or contracts that are no longer valid. The latter have a simple informative power, and not a normative one, although they can regain some such power in a new sort of context – as when in a judicial context an expired train ticket counts as an alibi for the defendant. The social object is dependent on minds for its beginning to exist, but once it has been recorded it acquires an independent existence, comparable in some ways to what holds in the case of physical artefacts, with the only important difference that a physical artefact can offer its affordance even in the absence of minds (a table can also be a shelter for an animal), while a document, typically, cannot.[8]

What I propose under the title of 'documentality' is thus a 'weak textualism' (that is, also a 'weak constructivism'): weak because it assumes that inscriptions are decisive in the construction of *social* reality, but – contrary to what we may define 'strong textualism', practiced by postmodernists – it excludes that inscriptions may be constitutive of reality *in general*. Weak textualism is therefore such because it results from the weakening of Derrida's thesis that 'there is nothing outside the text', which is transformed into 'there is nothing *social* outside the text', in the two variants of strong document (constitution of an act) and weak document (recording of a fact). Weak textualism thus admits a moderate constructivism, which does not clash with the realistic intuition.

Thus it becomes possible to reconstruct deconstruction, assigning the realist intuition and the constructivist one each to their sphere of competence. This produces the following results:

1. Natural objects are independent of epistemology and make natural science true.
2. Ontology is independent of epistemology.
3. Social objects are dependent on epistemology, without being subjective.
4. 'Intuitions without concepts are blind' applies primarily to social objects (where it has a constructive value), and less to the epistemological approach to the natural world (where it has a reconstructive value).
5. The realist intuition and the constructionist intuition have therefore equal legitimacy in their respective fields of application.

Now, documental recording sustains normativity only against the background of some normative social practice. Banknotes become just so much waste paper if there is no institutional background to support them. In fact, if mere recording were enough for the existence of social objects, then the old European currencies would continue to be valid even when they are actually worth nothing because in the meantime their regulatory environment has changed. But if – as I shall articulate in the section dedicated to the emergence – documentality is the source of intentionality and normativity, then I think that this objection loses its validity, as evidenced by the fact that a collective amnesia (i.e. the disappearance of documentality) would coincide with the disappearance of intentionality and normativity. In other words, the institutional background that supports documentality is in turn a documental background, and so on *ad infinitum*.

Thus, the thesis that I defend here is rather that the dead letter is the condition of possibility of the living spirit, because the customs, languages and practices (i.e. documentality) are what allows for the development of intentionality, which would otherwise remain inert. Ultimately, what makes us give intentionality an intrinsic normative value is simply the fact that it is accompanied by a form of vitality: the letter is dead, the spirit is alive. But what is alive in the spirit, what makes it effective, is precisely the letter, the iteration. Quite simply: as Wittgenstein noticed, a private language is impossible,[9] therefore the expression of meanings comes from the iterability of the letters – which is equal to saying that the dead documental letter is the condition of possibility of the living intentional agent. Behind the assumption of the priority of intentionality over documentality there is a myth of understanding – a mythology that claims a unique and superior quality that characterises our (Western, analytical) consciousness and makes it into a manifestation of a living spirit, irreducible to a machine or to mere matter.[10]

But where would this difference between soul and automaton be? The highest artistic, spiritual and institutional functions can be carried out perfectly through an automated system. Is there any difference between the conductor, the priest who celebrates the Mass, or the President of the United States making the inaugural speech to Congress? The conductor and the priest follow an already written text, maybe the President pretends to be improvising, but the text was written for him by a ghostwriter.[11] Yet, in all of those cases, this should be the climax, the focus, the appearance of the spirit on the cosmic-historical scene. All in all, the invocation to the goddess at the beginning of the Homeric poems, the idea that the poet merely gives voice to a text that comes from someone else, has the merit of recognising the extrinsic and automatic action lying at the heart of creation.

It may be objected that the examples I have made, referring to spiritually intense moments but still with a strong institutional or ritual characterisation, must necessarily refer to formulas, and therefore are not conclusive. Well, here too, it seems to me extremely problematic to distinguish between interior and exterior, institutional and non-institutional, form and substance. Let me explain. No one has ever doubted that true feelings can be expressed through hendecasyllables and triplets, but it is obvious that the use of these forms is an automatism. It is not implausible to imagine that someone, to express a radical feeling perceived as authentic, should resort to the triplet – just as, to express sympathy or indignation, we resort to clichés or to the formulas of subpoenas. Likewise, the form of confession presents us with rhetorical codified formulas[12] instead of the spontaneous total disclosure that we might expect: those of Augustine, Rousseau and Nietzsche are quite openly staged, but one could hardly argue that they are insincere.

Society

As regards society, documentality has also an immediate heuristic advantage. A theory of mind-dependence will always have intrinsically obscure aspects because it does not entail a simple causal dependence. For social objects to exist, it is necessary that there are at least two minds, though of course in complex social phenomena many more may be involved. In such cases many of those who are involved do not think in any way about the social object in the bringing into being of which they are involved, while still somehow managing to influence the process. At the same time there may be many others who do think about it, and yet are unable to exert such influence (think of a financial crisis, or a war). Apparently, we are dealing with a puzzle: social objects, as we have seen, are dependent on minds, but they are independent of knowledge (and even of consciousness): there may be a recession even though no one suspects it.

How is this possible? Does this not mean that social objects are both dependent on and independent of the mind? No, it does not. The contradiction would present itself only if 'mind dependence' were understood as dependence on one mind, as if any single person could determine the course of the social world. But a single mind does not make the laws, nor does it set the prices. Moreover, there are circumstances where our own mind seems to act independently of itself, as when we develop obsessive thoughts that we would rather not have.

If we no longer have a contradiction between 'dependence on the mind' and 'independence from knowledge', we still have to explain how social objects can persist even when we do not have consciousness or knowledge of them. That is why I argue that the foundation of the social world is documentality. In fact, when dealing with social objects we do not deal with a series of intentional acts that consciously keep the pertinent object alive, so to speak, as if we all thought at the same time about (say) the Constitution of the Republic of Italy. It is not so: the Constitution is written and ratified, and from that point on it is valid even if no one thinks about it (which in fact happens all too often).

In addition to helping us solve the puzzle of mind-dependence and -independence, the theory of documentality allows us also to provide a more solid basis for the constitutive rule proposed by the most influential theorist of social objects, John Searle: namely the rule 'X counts as Y in C' (physical object X counts as social object Y in context C). The limit of Searle's rule is twofold. On the one hand, it does not seem able to account for complex social objects (such as corporations) or entities lacking a physical foundation (such as debts). On the other hand, it makes the entirety of social reality depend on the action of an entity that is (in contrast to documents) completely mysterious, namely 'collective intentionality', which is, on Searle's account, responsible for transforming the physical into the social.

According to the version that I propose, on the contrary, it is very easy to account for the totality of social objects, from informal promises to businesses and even entirely non-physical entities such as debts and rights. In all these cases there is a minimal structure, which is guaranteed by

1 the presence of at least two people who commit some act (which may consist of a gesture, an utterance, or an act of writing) that
2 has the essential characteristic of being recorded on some support, even if this be only human memory.

In addition to accounting for the physical basis of the social object – which is not an X available for the action of collective intentionality, but a recording that can take place in multiple ways – the rule that I propose (and which I call the 'rule of documentality' as opposed to the 'rule of intentionality') has the advantage of not making social reality depend on a function, i.e. collective intentionality. In fact, such function is dangerously close to a purely mental process: this led Searle to make a statement that is anything but realist, namely that the economic crisis is largely the result of imagination.[13] From my perspective, on the contrary, being a form of documentality, money is anything but imaginary, and this circumstance allows us to draw a distinction between the social (what records the acts of at least two people, even if the recording takes place in the minds of those people and not on external documents) and the mental (which can take place only in the mind of a single person).

Of course, as we have said earlier, the Italian Constitution applies even if nobody thinks about it, but it ceases to have any significance if there is no one who is able to read it and to follow its dictates. The validity of what is written in a document remains dependent on systems of practices that makes the content of the document normative. Otherwise, it would be impossible to distinguish between a binding constitution and a constitution that is no longer in force, since both are written down somewhere. The theory of documentality, if taken to an extreme, could risk our not being able to explain this fundamental distinction. At this point, however, it is worth pointing out that the social cannot be merely 'that which records acts involving at least two people'. It must also include the practices that support this recording and make it valid and normative. That is precisely what I now propose to illustrate through the thesis of the emergence of intentionality and normativity from documentality. This is intuitively known by every advertising investor, who hopes that the iteration of a message will generate desires and lifestyles (i.e. intentionality and normativity) related to the advertised product.

Furthermore, the recourse to collective intentionality carries out a neutering of politics, while the call for documentality shows the inherent political nature of every social act. By 'neutering' I simply mean what follows. We wonder what the foundations of society might be and the answer, following a long philosophical tradition, can be: will to power, class conflict, fear, history, the friend–foe polarity. In the same way we wonder what the extreme social situations (i.e. those that can never be deleted from the set of possibilities) might be. We can answer, once again following a long tradition: order, slavery, exploitation, the Final Solution. Yet Searle's answer is: the basis of society is collective intentionality, which develops through the collective imposition of a function to things that originally did not have that function. Which is like saying that collective intentionality is the physiological basis of politics.

Let us ask a question: in what cases does such a system work? The main example, following what happened with Duchamp's ready-mades, is that of the art world, in which we decide to confer to a painting (or occasionally to a urinal) the honorific status of 'masterpiece'. Yet, significantly, such an operation turns out to be much more difficult with money. I might convince someone to regard my painting as a work of art and buy it, but I would hardly accept being paid by them in home-made money. If I did that, I would act like in the nineteenth-century sketch that appears in the introduction to the Italian edition of *Making the Social World*, where they try to persuade a girl to substitute milk with a document saying 'this is milk'.

Now, in order to be willing to confer the status of work of art to an artefact, there has to be a good deal of cooperation and disinterest, and this seems to be the character of all the social situations that Searle uses as examples: to play football, to be part of an orchestra, to collaborate in sport and recreational activities. Still, it seems utterly inadequate for describing purely endured situations, such as deportations and exterminations. With regards to this it is worth developing two considerations.

First. Searle presents us with the prototype of collective intentionality through the drawing of two heads saying 'we intend'. Of course, we can imagine situations in which this 'we intend' is realised in just this fashion; but those would still be exceptions compared to most social circumstances, which may range from disagreement to the radical subordination of an individual intentionality to other intentionalities, as in all situations involving coercion, to simple cases where employees work, semi-reluctantly, for pay. The social nature of Searlean collective intentionality, in contrast, seems to be confined to the sort of playful and disinterested cooperation that is involved, for example, in dancing, or rearranging furniture, and most importantly, it lacks one element essential to any social ontology, which is the ability to account for conflict.

Second. Following a line of reasoning not too different from that of Searle, Margaret Gilbert has located in 'walking together' the paradigm of being together as a community, and thus as the model of collective intentionality.[14] When a couple is taking a walk, their action can undoubtedly be the expression of a shared intentionality. But let's picture now soldiers marching in goose step. Is that, too, a case of collective intentionality? Or imagine a group of soldiers who are prisoners-of-war, marching at the command of their captors. Do we have here a case of what we might call 'marching together'? That there is an analogy between this last case and the other two is at least questionable. And don't forget that, without falling into an excessive pessimism, the way in which we normally interact in a society is in some ways like that of prisoners – certainly not under the threat of a gun pointed at our heads, but still within the boundaries set by laws, street signs, fees, prohibitions.

It is true that Searle claims that war is also part of a collective intentionality, but this seems to reflect – to give an Italian example – the military enthusiasm of 1915 Italy's entrance in the war rather than the 1917 massacres, when death threats were necessary to keep soldiers fighting. One would say that Searle, at least in the explicit form of his theory, lacks the element that led Clausewitz to say that war is the prosecution of politics – and, in fact, one of the features of war, perhaps the main one, is that it carries on even when all enthusiasm is gone and orders are obeyed in robot-like way, through duty or fear.

The sociality defined by collective intentionality seems thus to be that of a Schillerian cooperation ('man is only fully a human being when he plays') immune from conflicts. Society becomes a sort of barbecue weekend in a Californian suburb: you take care of the sandwiches, I'll bring the beers, he'll be the cook, she's the party queen and so on.[15] Also, it is really hard to understand, from Searle's perspective, what difference there is between political approval and the appreciation for food, a film, or a best-selling novel. Searle locates at the heart of social activity a kind of cooperation and a shared acceptance that, in the best-case scenario, reflect an idealised and modern attitude (it is inconceivable in a feudal society, for instance). It is a world where power relations seem not to exist. But the truth is that power relations do exist: they simply can't be seen.

The insufficiency of collective intentionality as the basis of the social is particularly evident in situations that show a lack of consensus. The example of a crumbling social reality through the dissolving of intentions is, for Searle, that of the 1968 uprisings at Berkeley. Now, to see a student uprising as the model of revolution or even war is not very different from regarding Duchamp or Truman Capote as the paradigm of the revolutionary. In fact, throughout this student uprising, professors stayed professors and kept getting their pay check, and the next year all was gone, unlike what happens in true revolutions. As for the 'campus war',[16] it was obviously a metaphor. A true change does not take place when intentionality varies, but rather when the transformation is fixed through documentality, in a series of acts with a political value.

Intentionality

If postmodernists have claimed, with a constructionist hyperbole, that fiction cancels reality, I say that intentionality derives from documentality. The prospect of documentality begins with the theory that – from its ancient to its modern supporters – conceives of the mind as a *tabula* on which to lay inscriptions. In fact, as we have seen, inscriptions have a powerful role in social reality: social behaviours are determined by laws, rituals and norms; social structures and education form our intentions.

These considerations can be easily supported by a simple thought experiment. Imagine some Crusoe figure, the first or last man on the face of the earth. Could our Crusoe be devoured by the ambition to become an admiral? A billionaire? A court poet? Certainly not, just as he could not sensibly aspire to follow trends, or to collect baseball cards or still-life paintings. And if, say, he tried to fabricate a document, he would be undertaking an impossible task, because to produce a document there must be at least two people, the writer and the reader. In fact, our Crusoe would not even have a language, and one could hardly say that he would 'think' in the usual sense of the term.[17] And it would seem difficult to argue that he was proud, arrogant or in love, for roughly the same reason why it would be absurd to pretend that he had friends or enemies.

Now, a good objection to the mind-*tabula* could be the following question: are we really talking about inscriptions or is it just a metaphor? An inscription in the strict sense is semantically inert and has meaning only if interpreted by some subjects endowed with intentionality. Provided that the mind is a *tabula* of inscriptions, if inscriptions are inert then we must postulate an intentional subject who interprets them; but if inscriptions are not inert and point to their own meaning, then they are themselves equipped with intentionality. So documentality as a theory of mind seems to assume, in any case, some notion of intentionality. A strategy to recover documentality as the foundation of intentionality could be to conceive the 'inscriptions' on the mind-*tabula* as inherently intentional 'mental files'.[18] In this case mental documentality would function as a memory whose inscriptions, unlike the inscriptions on paper, are intrinsically intentional.

So far, so good. But how would this 'mental intentionality' be different from the 'myth of understanding', i.e. the idea that vitality is the condition of understanding? Conversely, imagine the experience of reading a ciphertext: in what sense is intentionality the condition of understanding? It is a necessary but not sufficient condition, just as recording and documentality are. In short, there is no reason in the world to give primacy to intentionality as opposed to documentality. The first has only the characteristic of living, ensuring competence, but not immediately understanding, which rather derives from the sediment layers of documents.

There is another point that deserves consideration about the myth of understanding. On almost all occasions, far from negotiating or offering consensus, we follow norms without thinking about them, or questioning them, or even – and this is very common, as well as being presupposed by the law – without agreeing on (or to) them. We follow the rules 'blindly'. Here is the distinctive feature of our relation with the world. Just as nobody needs to know the functioning of a lift in order to use one, so very few people need to know the norms they adhere to. They are instilled by education and habit and live on behind the scenes. In all but the most exceptional circumstances (such as revolutions), social reality is, far from being actively constructed, passively undergone. It is this which lies at the basis of our ordinary assumption that money has an intrinsic value, that the police have the right in certain circumstances to confiscate one's driving license. Perhaps eventually, in some cases and for some people, there can be a moment of awareness. Yet this is merely a possibility that could never actually take place, and it certainly does not constitute the rule of being in the social world – let alone being its presupposition.

Thus, on the one hand, the mind cannot arise unless it is immersed in the social, made up of education, language, communication and recording of behaviours. On the other hand, there is the huge category of social objects. Rather than sketching a world at the subject's disposal, the sphere of social objects reveals the inconsistency of solipsism: the fact that in the world there are also others in addition to us is proven by the existence of these objects, which would have no *raison d'être* in a world where there were only one subject. There is no thought without social normativity, nor is there normativity without the social.[19] This brings me to my second argument: namely that normativity derives from documentality.[20]

Emergence

In this regard I would like to suggest two reflections. The first concerns the externalism of meaning, which seems to be fully realised in the Web. The conception of the environment as a sphere in which emergence takes place proposes a Copernican revolution whose basis is the thesis, brought forward by Wittgenstein, that 'meaning is use'.[21] Let me explain. The world as a whole is a huge pool of competence without understanding, and no meaning is given 'in itself', but always and only in relation to other meanings. If this is the case, functions such as intentionality and normativity may only take place in an environment that progressively develops documentality. We must therefore imagine a long chain of being that, through interaction, gradually leads to the emergence of everything, including taxes and holidays. This has become particularly evident in the boom of documentality the age of the Web.

I wish to draw attention to this point by suggesting an equivalence between society and media in the age of the Web. Of course it could be argued that between society and media there is at least a quantitative difference. The media seem to ensure a much larger degree of iterability, replicability and instantiability than society, in the strict sense. The media might be seen as a powerful enhancement of the documental structure that constitutes society. The media introduce iteration methods that are more and more refined (notational rather than purely mechanical) and increasingly pervasive (with phonography, photography and cinema one can not only iterate conceptual contents, but also perceptual ones).

Yet, what this objection does not seem to take into account is that, with the new media, the difference between society and media completely disappears. For now the same technical devices are delegated to the production of entities on both sides of the divide. With the same tablet you can buy a plane ticket or earn a diploma, watch a sports event or write a restaurant review. Here there seems to be the outline of a dialectic: first is the pre-media (ante-Gutenberg) phase, then is the classical (post-Gutenberg but ante-Jobs) phase, and finally is the social media (post-Jobs) phase in which we now live.

The Web is a recording system that generates a superorganism that evolves autonomously, just like a termite mound, which structures complex articulations in the total absence of a central system.[22] Now, in the light of the Darwinian theory of the mind proposed by Daniel Dennett,[23] we might ask ourselves: is it not exactly the same thing for the human brain? Just like ants (or like computer memories and the whole Web), single neurons do not 'think', but 'download'. Yet the whole of them constitutes consciousness and thought.

Now, I do not mean at all to consider the Web as some sort of macro-consciousness or macro-brain, with yet another restatement of the thesis – which in retrospect proved to be fallacious – that the Web is a 'collective intelligence'.[24] I simply assert that the Web, as a macro-archive and macro-community, presents the same mechanism that takes place in superorganisms or in intelligence (natural or artificial), so that organisation precedes and produces understanding. From this point of view, one could even speak of a *computer evolutionism*, which depends on computers much more than it depends on designers. Computers have evolved independently from our original previsions, revealing the real needs of society: a calculation tool turned into an archive tool, an isolated machine became a machine connected to the Web. Something similar also happened with the mobile phone, which was thought of as a tool to talk but tuned into a writing device, with the ultimate convergence between mobile phone and computer (in smartphones and tablets).

It is in the environment of documentality that the 'we' takes place, through the genesis of what I have proposed we call documental community.[25] Again, we are dealing with a difference with respect to collective intentionality, regarded as a sort of natural primitive instinct that makes us say 'we' instead of 'I' in a number of situations, and that is the basis of the construction of the social world. I have several doubts in regard to this, because in fact the 'we' is only reached through training. As I tried to explain earlier, it is true that a group of people on a trip can say 'we are walking', but is it still 'collective intentionality' when those who are walking are a group of prisoners held at gunpoint? In the perspective of documentality, it is through the sharing of documents and traditions that a 'we' is constituted.[26]

It is precisely for this reason that society has adopted writing and archives so early: in order to ensure that the spirit can manifest itself and become recognisable, gaining visibility and permanence in time. From this point of view, the most transparent form of the 'we' is a document bearing signatures and exhibiting with honesty the terms, boundaries and objectives of the 'we' that in this version appears as the conscious agreement between a defined number of people for a specific purpose. Of course one could argue that this kind of sharing requires that the 'we' should be already constituted. But here I would like to point out that the process I described does not constitute a rigid and unidirectional determination so that documentality leads to the 'we', but rather a virtuous circle for which collective interaction (sharing, made possible by iterations, recordings, imitations and education, i.e. various forms of documentality) supports the production of documents that enhances collective interaction itself, which in turn enhances the production of documents.

To put things in a more all-encompassing way, along the lines suggested by the German mediologist and philosopher Friedrich Kittler, it is not so much the case that the media are an extension of man as that man is himself a product of the media. This thesis is all the more convincing given that, as I want to suggest, any difference in principle between society and the media has ceased to be. We could say (considering the human being as intrinsically normative) that documentality is the source of normativity, and not the opposite. Everything that becomes powerful can follow its own logic;[27] the more general thesis is that any system for emancipation is at the same time a system for control. Machines emancipate people from physical fatigue but deliver them up to industrial work. The Internet appeared at its outset as a liberation from the world of work and as a new countervailing power; in reality, however, it introduced a new layer of work and a new sort of power. This takes nothing away from the merits of the Internet, just as the assembly line takes nothing away from the merits of the machines it uses. But still it is an element that cannot be underestimated. This is the dark and deep side of the Web, which we need to make explicit.

Surprisingly, the greatest thinkers of the power of the Internet are, in my opinion, two figures that have never known it, and perhaps not even suspected its future existence: Schmitt, who emphasised that the essence of power lies in bureaucracy, and Jünger, who theorised the total mobilisation and militarisation as the essence of the modern world. The action of documentality over intentionality thus manifests itself as speed, conflict, normativity and, ultimately, mobilisation and responsibility.[28]

Responsibility

It is not true that 'the Internet makes you stupid', as argued by Nicholas Carr with excessive pessimism. What is happening is rather a transformation of culture.[29] The basic idea is this: the two pages, the paper one and the web page, are not the same for many obvious reasons, one of which is particularly crucial. The paper page invites silence and concentration, the web page suggests connection and distraction. Should the web page finally dispel the paper page, this would not be the end of intelligence or education, but only the end of that field of concentration that was high culture in the Western tradition. In fact, what are the characteristics of fast thought in the age of the Web? First of all, the loosening of inhibitions. Or at least a primacy of emotion over logic, in agreement with Daniel Kahneman's thesis in *Thinking, Fast and Slow*.[30] But – this time following Bourdieu,[31] who referred to fast-thinkers by necessity – the greatest risk of premature speculation is stereotype. The self-injunction to hurry is often a compulsion to repeat, with the result that fast-thought is systematically old-thought, something well-known (that is maybe even wrong).

As for conflict, in social networks there is the transcendental illusion that the same tool, the text message or the email used for very private communications, is at the same time the means for the most official and public ones. In this way, the very distinction between public and private – or rather, between universal and intimate – collapses, perfecting a mechanism that was already under way at the time of the mass media, but that previously only referred to famous people, whereas today it regards everybody. Furthermore, in the Web everything is created, nothing is destroyed and everything is recycled, so that an inaccurate or inappropriate comment made without thinking can travel round the world. As a result, the Web, much more than public opinion (which necessarily passes through at least the censorship arising from the belief that there are things you cannot say), serves nowadays as our collective unconscious,[32] extremely argumentative and aggressive.

Nevertheless, the most important aspect, in my opinion, is the way in which documentality becomes a source of normativity. If it were not possible to keep traces, there would be no mind, no thought, and no intention. But without the possibility of inscription there would not even be social objects, starting from the fundamental case of the promise. And, if this is so, then perhaps we should translate Aristotle's sentence that 'man is a *zoon logon echon*' as: 'man is an animal endowed with inscriptions', or rather (since one of the meanings of logos in Greek is precisely 'promise', 'given word') as: 'man is an animal that promises'. To quote Nietzsche: 'The breeding of an animal that *can promise* – is not this just the very paradox of a task which nature has set itself in regard to man?'[33]

From recording thus derives a mobilisation and especially a total responsibilisation. The Internet is an empire on which the sun never sets: at any time we can receive a request for work to be done, and at all times we are responsible for responding to such requests, in a process that extends indefinitely the duration of work and the dominion of responsibility (because all the requests are recorded). Imagine life with an old type of phone, the kind without a memory. If it rang when we were not at home, we would remain blissfully unaware of the call that we had missed. We lived on, happily and obligation free. Today each 'missed call' is recorded on our phone, and generates an obligation to respond, raising the pang of guilt in what we call 'soul'. The very fact of recording makes us responsible: a promise made between people without memories would not be a promise; it would be a series of empty words. This is why the world is filled with paper, files, archives and registries. Moral responsibility, at its core, is just this: inscription and recording. It is not by chance that divine omniscience is represented as the holding aloft of a book, in which everything is written and nothing is forgotten.

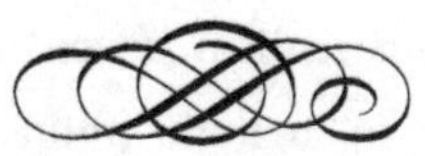

Afterword
The coral reef of reality: new philosophical realisms

Sarah De Sanctis
(London Graduate School/LabOnt)
Vincenzo Santarcangelo
(University of Turin/LabOnt)

Introduction

The aim of this chapter is to expose the core theoretical features of what can be regarded as a return to realism after a period of prevailing antirealism. The main common trait of all *post*-postmodern realists is indeed the wish to 'return' to realism after the hegemony of antirealism characteristic of postmodernity.[1] In fact, to follow Graham Harman, 'no one in the continental tradition was declaring realism *devoid of ironic etymological tricks* prior to 2002'.[2] In analytic philosophy things were no different: as noted by Maurizio Ferraris,[3] Donald Davidson claimed that one does not encounter perceptions, but beliefs,[4] and Nelson Goodman asserted that the word is constructed the same way as a work of art.[5] The French philosopher Quentin Meillassoux pertinently summarised the situation when he stated that 'in continental philosophy . . . we can't see the problem of the truth of reality. And in analytic philosophy there is so much realism that they can't be amazed by the capacity of realism. This is maybe just a caricature, but that's my impression.'[6]

In addition to their wish to overcome postmodern antirealism, new realists – as we shall call them for the purposes of this chapter – share some other significant traits. As regards the *pars destruens*, the main common feature of these thinkers consists of a rejection of what Meillassoux has efficaciously called 'correlationalism': these philosophers drastically reduce the importance of human thought and conceptual schemes while strongly reaffirming the brute objectivity of the world. As for the *pars construens*, there are two main threads: on the one hand there is a re-evaluation of common sense and perception (as is carried out by Maurizio Ferraris, partly following Umberto Eco,[7] and the later Hilary Putnam); on the other hand there is a much more counter-intuitive approach, so to speak, which has been labelled 'Speculative Realism'.

The name 'speculative realism,' which later became that of an entire philosophical movement (although a very vaguely defined one), was originally the title of a conference held at Goldsmiths

College in London on 27 April 2007. The moderator of the conference was Alberto Toscano, and among the invited speakers there were Ray Brassier (from the American University in Beirut), Iain Hamilton Grant (from the University of the West of England), Graham Harman (from the American University in Cairo) and Quentin Meillassoux (from the École Normale Supérieure in Paris). Apparently the authorship of the name should be ascribed to Brassier, though Meillassoux had already used the term 'speculative materialism' to describe his own philosophical position. A second conference, entitled 'Speculative Realism/Speculative Materialism', took place at the University of the West of England, in Bristol, on 24 April 2009. This time, the speakers were Ray Brassier, Iain Hamilton Grant, Graham Harman and Alberto Toscano replacing Quentin Meillassoux, who could not attend.[8]

Despite the successful dedicated conferences, later (in an interview published in March 2011 in *Kronos* magazine) Brassier himself categorically denied that there is anything like a movement called 'speculative realism': 'The "speculative realist movement" exists only in the imaginations of a group of bloggers promoting an agenda for which I have no sympathy whatsoever: actor-network theory spiced with pan-psychist metaphysics and morsels of process philosophy.' Brassier went even further in this interview, claiming that the internet cannot provide a suitable place for serious philosophical debate: 'I do not believe it is acceptable to try to concoct a philosophical movement online by using blogs to exploit the misguided enthusiasm of impressionable graduate students. … I see little philosophical merit in a "movement" whose most signal achievement thus far is to have generated an online orgy of stupidity.'

On the other hand, in a recent article that summarises the present state of health of speculative realism[9], Graham Harman writes that not only does speculative realism exist, but it is also worthy of capital letters, being the proper name of a current of thought recognised in academia and beyond:

> Speculative Realism is now the topic of a thriving book series at a major university press, and the subject of at least one forthcoming monograph. It is embedded in the editorial policy of several philosophy journals. It has become a *terme d'art* in architecture, archaeology, geography, the visual arts, and even history. It has crossed national boundaries with ease, and is surely the central theme of discussion in the growing continental philosophy blogosphere.

Indeed, these new forms of realism have been very influential in a series of extra-disciplinary areas such as law, historiography, pedagogy, literary criticism, geography, economics, media and computer studies, linguistics, architecture, political science, art and music.[10]

For the purposes of this chapter, we will focus on speculative realism (as it is developed by Quentin Meillassoux and Graham Harman) and commonsense realism (as it is developed by Hilary Putnam and Maurizio Ferraris). There are obviously other kinds of realism available on the philosophical arena, such as external realism or scientific realism, as well as several thinkers that we will not have the space to consider in this short essay – for example, despite their relatively loose attachment to speculative realism, we will not address Iain Hamilton Grant's recovery of later Schelling's thought[11] and Ray Brassier's transcendental nihilism.[12] Our choice of philosophers is certainly arbitrary to an extent,[13] but we do think it will allow us to provide the reader with a good theoretical overview of post-postmodern realism that, despite being far from comprehensive, will make it possible to answer with a good degree of approximation the question 'what is *post* in post-postmodern realism?'

Beyond access: correlationalism rejected

Levi Bryant's *The Democracy of Objects* begins as follows: 'For my daughter Elizabeth, so that you might always remain curious and remember that it is not all about us.'[14] The last part of this dedication is the gist of the starting point of all the thinkers we will consider: that is, 'it is not all about us'. According to them, in fact, there is a world that exists independently of human thought, which is therefore knocked off the pedestal where Kantian philosophy had placed it. In order to clarify this concept, it might be useful to briefly retrace the philosophical history of what Quentin Meillassoux defined 'correlationalism'.

Ferraris claims that the forefather of correlationalist philosophy was probably René Descartes: he was responsible for distinguishing between *res cogitans* and *res extensa* – to put it in simple terms, between thought and objects. In his view, these two spheres are forever separated, and the gap between them can only be bridged by God. It is worth noting that Descartes' starting point is a strong distrust of the senses: sensual perception can deceive, it does not offer *certain* knowledge, and it should therefore be dismissed. The only thing we can be certain about is our own thought, from which we then derive our existence: *cogito ergo sum* – being depends on thought. Thus, thought is the first immediate object of our experience, and we have no contact with the world 'out there', that is, unless through the mediation of thought.

This schism was destined to persist throughout centuries of philosophy and was radicalised in Kant's famous Copernican Revolution, which well-deserved its name as it radically changed the way of considering knowledge. In fact, whereas it was commonly thought, up to then, that human cognition conforms to objects, Kant posited that objects must conform to our cognition instead: the structure of human mind shapes all experience, thus acquiring an active role in the construction of reality. This move, once again, has to do with perception: Kant, in fact, was trying to solve the problem of how it was possible to get a priori knowledge of the sensible world; if all knowledge derives from experience, but the latter is structurally uncertain, it is necessary to found experience by resorting to a priori structures that will stabilise its aleatory character.

Many authors have noted that, despite its name, there is little Copernicanism to Kant's revolution: if we consider that he is placing the subject at the centre of the universe, it has a rather poignant Ptolemaic character.[15] The fundamental consequence of this move is that the human–world relation assumes a fundamental role. This approach, which still dominates philosophy today, is the main polemical target of new realisms. We shall now look at how the authors we have chosen to focus on set themselves against such a view.

Graham Harman, in his recent book *The Quadruple Object*, devotes a whole section to the idea of an Anti-Copernicus. In a previous article, he summarised Kant's philosophical position by saying that the famous philosopher makes two basic claims: (1) Human knowledge is finite, since things-in-themselves can be thought of but never known. (2) The human–world relation (mediated by space, time, and the categories) is philosophically privileged over every other sort of relation; philosophy is primarily about human access to the world, or at least it must take this access as its starting point.[16] Now, Object-oriented Ontology (Harman's specific position within Speculative Realism) agrees with the first Kantian point and disagrees with the second,[17] because it posits that the things-in-themselves remain forever beyond our grasp, but not because of a specifically *human* failure to reach them. To support this point, he reads Heidegger's tool-analysis[18] – usually interpreted as a pragmatist theory – under a new light: in fact, he interprets Heidegger's claim that reality withdraws into hiddenness as the proof of the inadequacy of any relation: the relation between the I think and the object (or any kind of relation) is a distorted version of a real reality, so to speak, that remains inaccessible.

As for the second mistake made by Kant, Harman claims that instead, relations *in general* fail to gasp their *relata*, and in this sense the ghostly things-in-themselves haunt inanimate causal relations no less than the human–world relation, which no longer stands at the centre of philosophy. Thus, any kind of relation – whether between humans and objects, or between objects – is of equal importance: the human–world relation, which Kant regarded as crucial, is placed at the same level as any other, following Alfred North Whitehead's claim that 'all human and non-human entities have equal status insofar as they all *prehend* other things, relating to them in one way or another'.[19]

Another thinker who sets himself openly against Kant is Maurizio Ferraris. In his book entitled (significantly) *Goodbye Kant!*,[20] as well as is many of his other works, he argues for the need to abandon transcendentalism. Ferraris focuses on the problem of perception: from a Kantian perspective, knowledge does begin in the senses, but it does so only if the senses are fixed by conceptual schemes that are independent from experience and prior to it. In Ferraris' view, Kant thus paved the way to constructivism, the position according to which reality is constructed by human conceptual schemes and perceptual apparatuses. This view, though, he posits, should be applied mostly to certain aspects of social reality, and not to reality as a whole. Social reality does, in fact, largely depend on human beings and their practices, but physical reality is mostly independent of any kind of conceptuality, being brutally there. It could be argued that he also hints, loosely, at Heidegger's tool-analysis: Heidegger states that humans notice a tool when it fails its task, while otherwise taking it for granted. Similarly, Ferraris posits that reality is *unamendable* and it is precisely when it proves to be so, when it surprises us and, so to speak, we crash against it that we realise just how independent it is from our thoughts and wishes.

The most influential argument against Kant's legacy was probably offered by Quentin Meillassoux in his book *Après la finitude* (2006, English translation *After Finitude*, 2008). What he opposes is the position of 'correlationalism,' namely: 'any current of thought which maintains the unsurpassable character of [correlation]', and: 'by correlation we mean the idea according to which we only ever have access to the correlation between thinking and being'.[21] In his view, this has had the negative consequence of the loss of the absolute, in the original meaning of the unrelated or unrelational, which is what he sets out to recover. He believes that what is crucial in correlationalism (and especially in Kant) is that 'the transcendental doesn't refute realism, it doesn't make it inconsistent, it makes it amazing – unthinkable but true. And that's what we have lost.'[22]

Meillassoux's attempt at recovering this lost absolute starts by bringing to the fore the so-called 'arche-fossil', namely the material support proving the existence of any reality anterior to the emergence of the human species or of any form of life in general. Reality was there first, before humans or any kind of life, and is therefore anterior to givenness itself. In other words, through the arche-fossil we can achieve what post-Kantian philosophy has always regarded as impossible, namely '*to get out of ourselves*, to grasp the in-itself, to know what is whether we are or not'.[23]

We hope that we have provided a sufficiently clear overview of how new realisms reject correlationalism and set themselves as a return to realism after the correlationalist hegemony, which culminated in postmodern antirealism. Yet it is important to note that these new forms of realism are, after all, new, in that they do not call for a return to classical or 'metaphysical' realism – the postmodern criticism to which they have internalised. They are rather – as noted several times by Maurizio Ferraris (through the concept of *resilience*) and Timothy Morton (broadening the scope of the discussion up to including an ecological perspective) – a series of philosophical positions united by powerful *family resemblances* that have emerged in this particular historical moment, at the convergence of certain cultural and historical contingencies. To use Robin Mackay's words:

> When I introduce the notion of speculative realism . . . I often remark how timely it is that this sort of philosophy should be emerging today, because the ecological stakes of what contemporary science tells us about the past and about the future precisely leads us to contemplate, in the title of Alan Weisman's recent book *The World Without Us*. Weisman's book describes in detail how long it will take for each of the products of human civilization to break down and disappear once we are gone. Now, evidently what's at stake in coming to terms with that reality is precisely to overcome correlationism.[24]

Let us now look at the new realist *pars construens*. We shall start by examining the view shared by those who emphasise the importance of perception and the so-called 'manifest image',[25] that is, the supporters of common-sense realism.

Why perception matters: common-sense realism

As we emphasised in the previous section, in the rejection of correlationalism there is a certain insistence on the role of perception. This view is endorsed by those thinkers that we are grouping here under the title of common-sense realists: in fact, this type of realism assumes that we have a direct access to the world, so that the information we get from our common sense (while not having epistemological primacy over the scientific discourse) should not be discarded – in fact, it is first of all common sense that tells us that there is *something* out there, escaping thought.

One of the strongest and earliest endorsers of this idea is Maurizio Ferraris, the above-mentioned author of the *Manifesto of New Realism*.[26] In fact, the Italian thinker has referred to perception as the means to go from aesthetics (understood in its original meaning of *aisthesis* — as sense-perception) to ontology. For Ferraris, perception, conceived as the set of sensory apparatuses through which we can become aware of the outside world, refers to Baumgarten's concept of aesthetics, defined as a 'science of sensory experience' and *analogon rationis*.[27] In this sense, aesthetics is a new discipline altogether, rather than a new definition of a discipline. It is elaborated on the basis of the distinction made by Leibniz between (1) obscure knowledge, which does not even allow for the identification of the perceived, and (2) clear knowledge, which instead achieves that goal. Clear knowledge is in turn is divided into (2.1) clear and confused knowledge, in which the single components of the perceived cannot be isolated, and (2.2) clear and distinct knowledge, in which those components are instead distinguished. The former kind (2.1), preliminary to the former, is largely present in the process of our continuous experience of the outside world. For Baumgarten, it is an essential prerogative of aesthetics. Compared to the fine arts and the perception of beauty, aesthetics is thus understood as a doctrine of sensible perception that reconciles two paths that until then had been separated: that of perceptology and psychology, and that of the precepts about art and beauty.

Ferraris investigates sensibility by addressing the problem of knowledge, paying particular attention to the finite character of human intellect.[28] Baumgarten resorted to an epistemological justification to explain the continuity between sensible and intelligible, whereas Kant had theorised a gap between those two spheres – a gap that was crucial to his system. Ferraris notes that by returning to Baumgarten's conception it is possible to understand the emergence of the 'physiognomy of an *episteme* that . . . responds to questions mostly addressed by other disciplines, be they theory of knowledge, psychology, phenomenology and ontology'.[29] Aesthetics, as Ferraris understands it, is not a 'science of sensible perception as such ... but a science of sensible perception as inscribed and kept, for example in the mind or in the imagination as a *tabula rasa*.'[30] He thus detaches aesthetics from its usual specific sphere – that of art – by saying that, on the contrary, one can recognise it even without having ever seen an artwork. Aesthetics is to be found in a sphere that 'primarily pertains to psychology, perceptology and ontology'.[31]

Ferraris also insists on the importance of perception in that it was much underestimated by correlationalist philosophy. As we have briefly outlined, the forefathers of correlationalism often looked with distrust at sensible knowledge. Descartes was the first to do this in modern philosophy, and Kant later radicalised his division between *res extensa* and *res cogitans*. In addition to them, Ferraris also speaks of Hume as one of the contributors to the birth of correlation (it is worth underlying this because, on the contrary, Meillassoux goes back to Hume in many respects) insofar as he doubted induction, based on sensible knowledge, which is never 100 per cent certain, and therefore rejected perception as such.

What Ferraris posits is that the underlying assumption of all these philosophers is that the senses should have an epistemological role – and that this assumption is wrong. In fact, the role of the senses is rather ontological: 'in a certain way, the function of perception is similar to Popper's falsification, except that here it has an ontological role rather than an epistemological one'.[32] Perception is the first area in which unamendability takes place, so that we should not know from perception what reality is, rather we should be using it as a barrier against our constructivist expectations to tell us what reality is *not*: that is, reality is not the mere correlation between interior thought and exterior materiality. Perception gives us an unamendable datum which 'may even be an error, a delusion, nonsense, but it certainly is something'.[33] This is the reason why, following the later Schelling, Ferraris defines his own position as 'positive realism': perception is the basis onto which we can build our knowledge of the world, since every negation orientates towards one or more *positive* determinations.[34]

Ferraris thus moves on to argue for the importance of distinguishing between ontology (what there is) and epistemology (what we know about what there is). So if reality is there independently of us, surprising us and often disappointing us, epistemology does depend on the human race and the correlation between thought and being. Therefore it is not true that, as constructivists posit, our concepts shape reality: objects possess independent features that put our knowledge to the test.

On this basis, Ferraris then draws a specific kind of ontological division: there are natural objects (which exist independently of conceptual schemes), ideal objects (which also exist independently of conceptual schemes) and social objects (which exist dependently on conceptual schemes). Ferraris wishes to limit the claims of constructivism (the view, following from Kantian correlationalism, according to which conceptual schemes construct the world) to the last class of objects. He sets himself sharply against postmodernism, a movement (if we may call it that) which he regards as marked by an extreme constructivism – as is seen, for instance, in Rorty's claim that 'nothing counts as justification unless by reference to what we already accept, and . . . there is no way to get outside our beliefs and our language so as to find some test other than coherence'.[35] Thus, in short, in social reality we have objects (such as money, marriages and professorships) that would cease to exist if human race were to disappear, but natural objects (such as mountains and rivers) would carry on just as before. Here Ferraris refers to a notion developed by Paolo Bozzi,[36] claiming that 'what emerges is a "naive physics" . . . the world presents itself to us as real'.[37]

A similar view is held by the later Hilary Putnam. The American philosopher famously went through several changes of perspective – from metaphysical realism to internal realism then to common-sense realism – which we do not have the space to look at.[38] Nevertheless, we wish to note that, precisely for this reason, the later Putnam is perhaps one of the most efficacious examples of what new realism is: in fact, he rejects internal realism (a vaguely Kantian position he previously endorsed, according to which truth is equal to intelligibility under ideal epistemic conditions) but he also rejects metaphysical or, if you wish, classical realism (according to which there is one true description of the world that can be grasped by the mind and philosophy, to quote Rorty, is 'the mirror of nature').

Upon closer inspection, one will realise that the main core of his re-thinking is not realism as such, but rather perception. In fact, in *Realism with a Human Face* he still focused on the crucial role of our mind and language as mediators of our relationship with reality, whereas in *The Threefold Cord: Mind, Body, and the World* he claims that 'the disaster is the idea that there has to be an interface between our cognitive powers and the external world'[39] thus arguing in favour of a direct relationship with the world, starting with perception. He obviously posits (as Ferraris also does) that perception is not infallible and should not be treated as the epistemological tool *par excellence*, but nonetheless he restores its importance to philosophy. As he recently stated, 'if we cannot explain how perception allows us to understand reality, every description of realism will be forever incomplete'.[40]

Putnam's re-evaluation of perception is nevertheless not incompatible with scientific realism. In fact, Putnam believes that there are different possible descriptions of the world, which are equally valid. This means that his common-sense realism, which, to put it simply, reasons in terms of tables and chairs, does not set itself against science and its talk of fermions and bosons. Among the possible languages, to carry on with the example of the chair, he also includes those of art or carpentry, with a position that vaguely reminds one of Markus Gabriel's hyperrealism.[41]

Yet he does insist on the fact that science provides an approximately correct description of the world. The argument he uses to defend this is well-known: it is the so-called 'miracle argument.'[42] Even if we accept that knowledge is forever bound to stay within the realm of language, surely we cannot see it as some randomly free-floating entity that is completely detached from the world and entirely self-referential (as posited by Quine and Rorty). How would prediction and scientific progress be possible? Indeed, there seems to be more than enough proof that there has been, in fact, a progressive accumulation of knowledge. As Ferraris put it, Rorty himself would certainly have preferred to be cured by a 2012 doctor rather than by Hippocrates.[43] Basically, if we deny the possibility that science does actually describe the world in an approximately right way, the only possible explanation for progress would be that of a miracle.

Once again, we have a very commonsensical position: while firmly rejecting the view that 'science is nothing but a system of conventions' that was 'particularly widespread within postmodernist circles',[44] Putnam does not claim that science is the only possible description of the world, nor that it is infallible: it is, as common sense suggests, approximately true and revisable. In the same way, while maintaining that perception is certainly not a primary epistemological tool, he reinstates its importance as the proof of our direct relationship to the external world, to which we do have unmediated access.

A much less commonsensical position is held by speculative realists[45] who, nevertheless, share the aim at reducing the importance of the human–world relationship and the role of human conceptual schemes while strongly asserting the brute objectivity of a world out there. So, in the next section we shall outline the specific views of Graham Harman and Quentin Meillassoux.

The object and the absolute: speculative realism

We have already mentioned thinkers who tend to drastically reduce the importance of the human–world relation. Perhaps no one does this more radically than Graham Harman: in fact, the American philosopher focuses his attention fully on the *object*, calling his philosophy precisely 'Object-oriented Ontology' (from now on OOO). At the basis of this specific declination of speculative realism there is, as in the philosophy of Maurizio Ferraris, a recovery of ontology. In the words of Timothy Morton:

'at a moment when the term ontology was left alone like a piece of well chewed old chewing gum that no one wants to have anything to do with, object-oriented ontology has put it back on the table'.[46] The underlying 'coral reef' of reality has always been there, it has never disappeared, and once we have discovered it we cannot pretend it does not exist. Furthermore, 'the entities in the reef – we call them "objects" somewhat provocatively – constitute all there is: from doughnuts to dogfish to the Dog Star to Dobermans to Snoop Dogg. People, plastic clothes pegs, piranhas and particles are all objects. And they are all pretty much the same, at this depth.'[47] At this level, then, there is no room to distinguish between life and non-life, nor between intelligent and non-intelligent beings. All these distinctions are made *by* humans *for* humans (it is what we call anthropocentrism). The mission of OOO is then 'to liberate autonomy for the sake of nonhumans'.[48]

According to OOO, in fact, objects have been somehow neglected throughout the history of philosophy, or rather – to use Harman's terminology – they have been either *undermined* (by thinkers who posited that there is something 'deeper' than the objects, such as some kind of one, ultimate reality) or *overmined* (by those who saw the objects as nothing more than the sum of their qualities, which gain relevance only when they are given a structure by the human mind). For our purposes, it is worth underlying that both metaphysical realism (there is one true reality beyond the specificity of objects) and scientific realism (only what is basic is real, that is, quanta and atoms) belongs to the first category of thinkers, while empiricists like

Hume (objects are just bundles of qualities) and transcendentalists like Kant (objects are given sense and structure only by the human mind) belong to the latter.

Harman structures his own position starting from Husserl, whom he defines as 'an object-oriented idealist'.[49] He obviously rejects Husserl's view that objects are considered (or are possible) only insofar as they appear, but he gladly insists on his focus on objects. In particular, he focuses on Husserl's revolutionary idea according to which objects are unified and covered by a multitude of shifting accidental qualities – this is the reason why a house, seen from different angles and perspectives, is still the same house. Husserl also distinguishes between those fleeting accidental qualities and the indispensable eidetic qualities, which the object needs in order to be what it is. The first qualities can be sensually experienced, the latter can only be inferred while never showing themselves entirely – and this is where Heidegger comes in. Harman resorts to tool-analysis and gives it a peculiar reading to demonstrate that objects (real objects, as opposed to Husserl's sensual objects) – much like tools – withdraw from human consciousness and can never be fully accessed.

The crucial point, though, is the following: 'the withdrawal of objects [does not] only afflict humans and a few smart animals, but expresses the permanent inadequacy of any relation at all'.[50] The specific way in which Harman opposes correlationalism, in fact, lies in 'dethroning' it and placing it among all kinds of relations – both between animals and objects, and between objects themselves. He then comes to elaborate a rather complex fourfold structure, according to which both real and sensual objects have both real and sensual qualities. The relations between each object and each quality generate time, space, *eidos* and essence. Real objects are inaccessible, and the only form of direct contact is between a real object and the corresponding sensual one.

We do not have the space to go into the details of Harman's metaphysics, but we wish to underline two aspects. The first is that Harman, in particular, sets his position against what he calls the 'Philosophy of Access'. The problem with this view, in Harman's opinion, is that it engages in a vicious circle – we cannot think something without thinking it. In other words, I cannot think of a tree as separated from my thought of it (as unthought) because if I think about it as unthought I am still thinking about it. In the same way, I can think of a tree (consider it) without thinking *it* (as apart from my own thinking of it, as an 'in-itself'). The underlying problem, we believe, is what Ferraris has defined as the confusion between ontology and epistemology: philosophers of access cannot imagine being outside of thought and confuse the thought of a tree with the tree itself. According to Harman, there *is* the tree-in-itself – only, we can access it solely through a 'parallax view', to borrow the title of Slavoj Žižek's book, and not directly.

The second aspect we wish to highlight is that, once again, there is a sharp rejection of Hume's thought. Harman talks about 'occasionalism' as all those kinds of philosophies, deriving from Descartes' division between *res cogitans* and *res extensa*, for which the gap between those two *res* is unbridgeable unless one resorts to God. Such a view is obviously not much in fashion today, but Harman points out that 'it is easy to laugh at occasionalists who say that all relations pass through God, but no one laughs when it is said that they all pass through human experience instead',[51] as Hume does. This point is worth underlining, we think, because all the philosophers we have looked at so far would definitely agree with Harman on this point.

A rather different position is assumed, instead, by Quentin Meillassoux, who takes Hume as one of the core thinkers in his philosophy. Meillassoux's position is the most radical one, in a way, and definitely the most counter-intuitive among all the new realists we are here considering. He can be seen as belonging to the new realist wave because of his rejection of correlation and his wish to 'get out of ourselves, to grasp the in-itself, to know what is whether we are or not',[52] but he does not do this in the name of a re-evaluation of perception, common sense, or the object. What he does, in a way, is very Cartesian: he dismisses sensible knowledge as illusionary and aims for the absolute. Let us clarify.

Meillassoux starts from the assumption that correlationalism – positing the impossibility of ever going beyond the relation between thought and being – has caused the loss of the absolute. As we have already mentioned, he starts from the idea of the ancestral and the arche-fossil – namely something that proves to be anterior to givenness itself – in order to break out of the correlationist circle. Then he retraces the origins of this loss of the absolute, and finds them in Kant's refutation of Cartesian thought. What is at stake is the principle of sufficient reason:

that is, the idea that everything has a reason and therefore there must be an ultimate, necessary cause for everything. In Descartes this cause was obviously God, but this way of thinking can be found in any metaphysics that claims that this or that entity 'must absolutely be ... whether it is Idea, pure Act, atom'[53] etc. Correlationalism disqualifies this view and rejects any idea of absolute necessity, so the problem is: how can one re-instantiate the absolute and the principle of sufficient reason without falling back into dogmatic metaphysics?

In order to achieve this goal, Meillassoux adopts the principle of facticity, according to which there are certain structures (laws of logics, causality and so on) that are fixed, but they constitute a fact rather than an absolute: their necessity cannot be grounded. So how can he reinstate the lost absolute, if the principle of facticity seems to disprove its existence even further? The next move Meillassoux makes is radical: he regains the absolute by absolutising the principle of facticity itself – the very principle by which correlationalism had rejected the possibility of an absolute. In other words, he posits that the absolute is to be found not in the correlation, but in the facticity of the correlation itself. To put it simply, he wants to demonstrate that the only necessity/absolute lies in contingency and that this view is presupposed by correlationalism itself.

Meillassoux does so by presenting the example of dogmatics arguing about what happens to the subject after his death. A Christian dogmatic claims that life goes on post-mortem, whereas the atheistic dogmatic posits the exact opposite. A correlationalist would object to both, and argue that these possibilities are equally possible, because there is no ultimate reason that would rule out one of the two options. The next step is crucial: Meillassoux moves from the correlationalist position, which claims that all options are possible and we do not know which is the right one, to the speculative one: we *know* that all options are possible and that is it. The point of adamant importance is that '*this capacity-to-be-other cannot be conceived as a correlate of our thinking . . . because it harbours the possibility of our own non-being*'.[54]

Now that we have regained the absolute as the necessity of contingency (and contingency alone), there remains the problem of how to make this fit with the presumed necessity of the laws of physics. This is where Hume comes into play (and where Meillassoux differs the most from other new realists): Meillassoux agrees with Harman in positing that what the senses give us is the mere illusion of stability as regards the physical world from which we illegitimately infer its necessity. In fact, he argues, we have no legitimate reason to believe that, say, gravity is *necessary*: it has merely worked so far. This does not entail that the laws of physics would have to change every minute or very often. It is true that, if we regard the universe as a totalisable infinity, it would seem simply mathematically improbable that a non-necessary law would not have changed in all this time. But Meillassoux resorts to Cantor's transfinity to show that the universe is not, in fact, totalisable and cannot be regarded as a greater Whole. Therefore, there is no ultimate reason to believe that the laws of physics would have changed often enough for us to notice.

In short, as counter-intuitive as it may seem, everything is contingent: there is no reason behind the universe, and there is something rather than nothing out of mere chaos. It is easy to see how Meillassoux's position departs both from naive realism and from scientific realism, and he might seem to have little to do with the new realist group. But as we said, regardless of the strategies adopted by the various thinkers, we believe they all share a starting point of significant importance: the wish to break out of correlation and to reach the thing-in-itself.

Conclusion

The philosophers we have looked at have very different positions. But a return to realism, as we hope to have made clear, can be retraced in all of the thinkers we have examined here, and in the many others (such as John R. Searle, Akeel Bilgrami and Paul Boghossian, to name just a few) we did not have the space to consider. In fact, these new derivations of realism share a wish to move beyond Kant's transcendental turn and its legacy in postmodern philosophy, but not through a return to something like metaphysical realism or dogmatic metaphysics. New realists want to reassert the importance of the external world (Ferraris and Putnam), the object (Harman and Morton) or the absolute (Meillassoux): in any case, they want to break out of the relation between thought and being and reach out beyond it, so as to demonstrate that, to refer once again to Bryant's expression, 'it is not all about us'.

Bibliography

Baumgarten, A.G., *Aesthetica/Ästhetik* (1750), edited by D. Mirbach, 2 vols, Hamburg: Felix Meiner Verlag, 2007.

Bozzi, P., *Fisica ingenua. Oscillazioni, piani inclinati e altre storie: studi di psicologia della percezione*, Milan: Garzanti, 1990.

Brassier, R., *Nihil Unbound. Enlightenment and Extinction*, London: Palgrave Macillan, 2007.

Bryant, L., *The Democracy of Objects*, Ann Arbor, MI: Open Humanities, 2011.

Davidson, D., *Inquiries into Truth and Interpretation*, Oxford: Oxford University Press, 1984.

De Caro, M. and Ferraris, M., eds, *Bentornata realtà*, Turin: Einaudi, 2012.

De Landa, M., *Intensive Science and Virtual Philosophy*, London: Continuum, 2002.

Eco, U., 'Di un realismo negativo', in M. De Caro and M. Ferraris eds, *Bentornata realtà*. Turin: Einaudi, 2012, 91–112.

Eco, U., *Interpretation and Overinterpretation*, Cambridge: Cambridge University Press, 1992.

Ferraris, M., *Estetica Razionale*, Milan: Raffaello Cortina, 1997.

Ferraris, M., 'Esistere è resistere', in Mario De Caro and Maurizio Ferraris (eds), *Bentornata Realtà*, Turin: Einaudi, 2012, 139–166.

Ferraris, M., 'Sum ergo cogito', in Emilio Carlo Corriero and Andrea Dezi (eds), *Nature and Realism in Schelling's Philosophy*, Turin: Accademia University Press, 2013a, 139–165.

Ferraris, M., *Goodbye Kant! What Still Stands of the Critique of Pure Reason*. New York: SUNY Press, 2013b.

Ferraris, M., 'Why perception matters', *Phenomenology and Mind* 4, 2013c, 55–56.

Ferraris, M., *Manifesto of New Realism*, New York: SUNY Press, 2014.

Gabriel, M., *Fields of Sense*, Edinburgh: Edinburgh University Press, 2014.

Gibson, J.J., *The Ecological Approach to Visual Perception*, Boston, MA: Houghton Mifflin, 1979.

Goodman, N., *Ways of Worldmaking*, Indianapolis, IN: Hackett, 1978.

Grant, I.H., *Philosophies of Nature After Schelling*, London: Continuum, 2006.

Harman, G., 'The current state of speculative realism', *Speculations* IV, 2013, 22–28.

Harman, G., *The Quadruple Object*. London: Zer0 Books, 2011.

Harman, G., 'The road to objects', *continent*, 1.3, 2011, 171–179.

Harman, G., *Tool-Being: Heidegger and the Metaphysics of Objects*. Chicago, IL: Open Court, 2002.

Mackay, R., http://www.urbanomic.com/Documents/Documents-1.pdf, p. 9 [Accessed 2 April 2014].

Meillassoux, Q., *After Finitude*, London: Continuum, 2008.

Meillassoux, Q., http://www.urbanomic.com/Documents/Documents-1.pdf, 22 July 2010, p. 10 [Accessed 2 April 2014].

Morton, T., 'Objects as temporary autonomous zones', *continent*, 1.3, 2011, 149–155.

Morton, T., *Realist Magic: Objects, Ontology, Causality*, Ann Arbor, MI: Open Humanity Press, 2013.

Putnam, H., *Realism with a Human Face*, Cambridge, MA: Harvard University Press, 1990.

Putnam, H., *Words and Life*, J. Conant, ed., Cambridge: Cambridge University Press, 1994.

Putnam, H., *The Threefold Cord: Mind, Body, and the World*, New York: Columbia University Press, 1999.

Putnam, H., 'Realismo e senso comune', in De Caro, M. and Ferraris, M. (eds), *Bentornata realtà*, Turin: Einaudi, 2012a, 5–20.

Putnam, H., 'Realismo sì o no? Sbagliava anche Russell', *La Stampa*, 4 December, 2012b.

Putnam, Hilary, 'On not writing off scientific realism', in H. Putnam, *Philosophy in an Age of Science*, Cambridge, MA: Harvard University Press, 2012c, 91–108.

Rorty, R., *Philosophy and the Mirror of Nature*, Princeton, NJ: Princeton University Press, 1979.

Sellars, W.S., *Science, Perception and Reality*, London: Routledge & Kegan Paul Ltd and New York: The Humanities Press, 1963.

Notes

Foreword

1 Immanuel Kant, *Critique of Pure Reason*, trans. Norman Kemp Smith (London: Macmillan, 1929), BXII–XIII.

2 Ian Hacking, *The Social Construction of What?* (Cambridge, MA: Harvard University Press, 1999), p. 24.

3 Immanuel Kant, *Opus postumum*, trans and ed. Eckart Förster (Cambridge: Cambridge University Press, 1993, p. 240).

4 Immanuel Kant, *Critique of Judgment*, Ak V: 177n. Trans. Werner S. Pluhar (Indianapolis, IN: Hackett, 1987, p. 16).

5 See Markus Gabriel, 'Is Heidegger's "turn" a realist project?', *Meta: Research in Hermeneutics, Phenomenology and Practical Philosophy*, Special Issue on New Realism, 2014b, 44–73. See also Ferraris' own contribution to that journal, M. Ferraris, 'New realism as positive realism', *Meta: Research in Hermeneutics, Phenomenology and Practical Philosophy*, Special Issue on New Realism, 2014, 172–213, and the excellent essay by Jocelyn Benoist, 'Reality', *Meta: Research in Hermeneutics, Phenomenology and Practical Philosophy*, Special Issue on New Realism, 2014, pp. 21–27.

6 Markus Gabriel, *Warum es die Welt nicht gibt*. Berlin: Ullstein, 2013. See also Markus Gabriel, *Fields of Sense* (Edinburgh: Edinburgh University Press, 2014).

7 Apart from the overt acknowledgment of the Hegelian input into the structure of the ensuing 'Introduction to New Realism', Ferraris has also written on Schelling 'Sum ergo cogito. Schelling and the positive realism', in Emilio Carlo Corriero and Andrea Dezi, eds, *Nature and Realism in Schelling's Philosophy* (Turin: Accademia University Press, 2014, pp. 187–201, and Kant *Goodbye, Kant!* Trans. Richard Davies (Albany, NY: SUNY, 2013). Gabriel is the author of numerous works on Schelling and German idealism, notably *Der Mensch in Mythos. Untersuchungen über Ontotheologie, Anthropologie und Selbstbewusststeinsgeschichte in Schellings 'Philosophie der Mythologie'* (Berlin: De Gruyter, 2006) and *Transcendental Ontology. Essays in German Idealism* (London: Bloomsbury, 2011). Although perhaps less true of Meillassoux, his 'Presentation' to the *Speculative Realism* workshop in London 2008 (in *Collapse* volume III (2007), pp. 408–435) works out his position against that of Fichte, while Hegel figures repeatedly in Q. Mellaissoux, *After Finitude* (London: Continuum, 2008).

8 See, e.g., John McDowell's 'Responses' to Pippin in Nicholas H. Smith, ed. *Reading McDowell on Mind and World* (London: Routledge, 2002), p. 277: 'Once my reminder of second nature has done its work, nature can drop out of my picture too.'

9 See Daniel Dennett's critique of Robert Brandom's *Making it Explicit*, 'The evolution of why', available at http://ase.tufts.edu/cogstud/dennett/papers/Brandom.pdf.

10 Hegel and particularly Schelling were both committed to a 'real-idealism' that in the first case *involved* a philosophy of nature, and in the second was premised on one. Fichte, as the self-proclaimed heir of Kant, is another matter, although some work has been done on his own philosophy of nature. See F. Scott Scribner's *Matters of Spirit. J.G. Fichte and the Technological Imagination* (Pennsylvania, PA: Pennsylvania State University Press, 2010) for a fascinating negotiation of the dichotomy of nature and artifice in Fichte's long engagements with the natural sciences.

11 This is clearly expressed, for example, in Schelling's *First Outline of a System of Naturephilosophy*, trans. Keith R. Peterson (Albany, NY: SUNY, 2003), p. 14: 'The concept of being as an originary substratum should be absolutely eliminated from the philosophy of nature . . . To philosophize about nature means *to create* nature.'

12 Kant, *Critique of Judgment*, describes the imagination's 'sacrifice' of its empirical use so as to gain a greater power according to 'a different law'.

13 Jean-François Lyotard, *Leçons sur l'analytique du sublime* (Paris: Galilée, 1991), p. 73.

14 Lyotard, *Leçons sur l'analytique du sublime*, p. 228.

15 John McDowell, *Mind and World* (Cambridge, MA: Harvard University Press, 1996), p. 85: 'I am suggesting that . . . we can keep nature as it were partially enchanted, but without lapsing into pre-scientific superstition or a rampant Platonism'. Here, McDowell's desideratum confirms both the accuracy and the stakes of Ferraris' diagnosis of the 'crisis in science'.

16 F.W.J. Schelling, 'Darlegung des wahren Verhältnisses der Naturphilosophie zur verbesserten Fichteschen Lehre', in *Schellings Werke*, ed. K.F.A. Schelling (Stuttgart and Augsburg: Cotta, 1856–61), XIV vols, here VII, 17. Schelling finds the essence of Fichte's opinion concerning nature to be 'that nature should be used, utilized, and that it only exists in order so to be used; the principle according to which he views nature is the economic-teleological principle.'

17 W.V.O. Quine, 'Two dogmas of empiricism', in W.V.O. Quine, *From a Logical Point of View* (Cambridge, MA: Harvard University Press, 1963), p. 44.

18 F.W.J. Schelling, *System der Weltalter*, ed. Siegbert Peetz (Frankfurt: Klostermann, 1998), p. 156. See also Ferraris, *Philosophies of Nature after Schelling* (London: Continuum, 2008).

19 F.W.J. Schelling, 'Stuttgart Seminars', in Thomas Pfau, ed. and trans. *Idealism and the Endgame of Theory. Three Essays by F.W.J. Schelling* (Albany, NY: SUNY, 1994), p. 197: 'To what extent is a system ever possible? I answer: long before man decided to create a system, there already existed one: the cosmos [*System der Welt*].'

20 Ferraris shares versions of 'naive physics' and, to an extent, the 'environment-involving' thesis of existence with Hilary Putnam, to whom he frequently refers. See Putnam, 'How to be a sophisticated "naïve realist"', in *Philosophy in an Age of Science* (Cambridge, MA: Harvard University Press, 2012), pp. 624–639.

21 On this point, see Paul W. Franks, *All or Nothing. Systematicity, Transcendental Arguments and German Idealism* (Cambridge, MA: Harvard University Press, 1995).

22 See Gabriel, 'Is Heidegger's "turn" a realist project?', p. 45.

23 Bernard Bosanquet, *The Principle of Individuality and Value* (London: Macmillan, 1912), p. 240. For his discussion of 'neo-idealism' and 'neo-realism', see especially chapter 1 of Bosanquet, *The Meeting of Extremes in Contemporary Philosophy* (London: Macmillan, 1923).

A few introductory remarks

1 Quentin Meillassoux, *Après la finitude. Essai sur la nécessité de la contingence* (Paris: Seuil, 2006).

2 Maurizio Ferraris, *Estetica razionale* (Milan: Raffaello Cortina, 1997). As Graham Harman has said: 'With some rare and ineffectual exceptions … no one in the continental tradition was declaring realism *devoid of ironic etymological tricks* prior to 2002'; Graham Harman, 'The current state of speculative realism', *Speculations: A Journal of Speculative Realism* IV (2013), p. 23. Harman has since very kindly acknowledged that he was unfamiliar with my work at the time of writing these words.

3 See M. Ferraris, *Manifesto of New Realism* (New York: SUNY Press, 2014b); M. Ferraris, *Where Are You? An Ontology of the Cell Phone* (New York: Fordham University Press, 2014c); M. Ferraris, *Goodbye Kant! What Still Stands of the Critique of Pure Reason* (New York: SUNY Press, 2013b); M. Ferraris, *Documentality. Why It Is Necessary to Leave Traces* (New York: Fordham University Press, 2012a).

4 The only other one being, to my knowledge, speculative realism, officially born in 2008 at a Conference in London, at Goldsmiths University (for more on this, see the Afterword).

5 For a full press review, see http://nuovorealismo.wordpress.com. For an analysis of the debate, see R. Scarpa, *Il caso Nuovo Realismo. La lingua del dibattito filosofico contemporaneo* (Milan-Udine: Mimesis, 2013).

6 See, for example, M. Ferraris, 'Nuovo Realismo', *Rivista di estetica* 48/3(2011), pp. 69–93, and M. Ferraris, *Manifesto del nuovo realismo* (Laterza: Roma-Bari, 2012d) (English translation *Manifesto of New Realism*).

7 Markus Gabriel, *Warum es die Welt nicht gibt* (Berlin: Ullstein, 2013) and M. Gabriel, *Fields of Sense. A New Realist Ontology* (Edinburgh University Press, Edinburgh 2014a).

8 Mauricio Beuchot and Josè Luis Jerez, *Manifiesto del nuevo realismo analógico* (Buenos Aires: Circulo Erméneutico, 2013).

9 See Ferraris, *Estetica razionale*. The topic of realism lies also at the centre of my conversations with Jacques Derrida. See Jacques Derrida and Maurizio Ferraris, *A Taste for the Secret* (Ithaca, NY and London: Cornell University Press, 2001).

10 M. Ferraris, 'The aging of the "school of suspicion"', in Gianni Vattimo and Pier Aldo Rovatti (eds), *Weak Thought* (New York: SUNY Press, 2012c). The Italian original dates back to 1983.

11 This emerges very clearly if you look at the forthcoming collection of writings (from 1978 to 1983), which includes the very first things I published at the age of 22 up until my contribution to *Weak Thought*. I chose to publish this collection because those papers are hard to find, but very useful to show the consistency of my position since my early years as a philosopher.

12 See, for instance, Q. Meillassoux, *Après la finitude. Essai sur la nécessité de la contingence* (Paris: Seuil, 2006); Ray Brassier, *Nihil Unbound. Enlightenment and Extinction* (London: Palgrave Macmillan, 2007); G. Harman, *The Quadruple Object* (London: Zer0 Books, 2011); Iain Hamilton Grant, *Philosophies of Nature after Schelling* (New York and London: Continuum, 2006). For a global overview, see Levi Bryant, Nick Srnicek and Graham Harman (eds), *The Speculative Turn. Continental Materialism and Realism* (Melbourne: re.press, 2011).

13 'We are not witnessing an end of writing which, to follow McLuhan's ideological representation, would restore a transparency or immediacy of social relations; but indeed a more and more powerful historical unfolding of a general writing', Jacques Derrida, *Margins of Philosophy* (Brighton: Harvester Press, 1982) p. 329.

14 The turn from metaphysical realism to internal realism (which is much more open to relativism) happened in Putnam precisely in the years of postmodernism, that is, between Hilary Putnam, *Meaning and the Moral Sciences* (London: Routledge and Kegan Paul, 1978) and H. Putnam, *Reason, Truth, and History* (Cambridge: Cambridge University Press, 1981b); the new realist perspectives can be seen in H. Putnam, *Renewing Philosophy* (Cambridge, MA: Harvard University Press, 1992). For an excellent presentation of Putnam's path through realism, see Mario De Caro, 'Il lungo viaggio di Hilary Putnam. Realismo metafisico, antirealismo e realismo naturale', *Lingua e stile* 4, 1996, pp. 527–545.

15 Umberto Eco, *Kant and the Platypus: Essays on Language and Cognition* (Boston, MA: Houghton Mifflin Harcourt, 1999), and already Umberto Eco, *The Limits of Interpretation* (Bloomington, IN: Indiana University Press, 1990).

16 Once again, I refer the reader back to Ferraris, *Estetica razionale*.

17 A vast treatise on this turn can be found in the collective volume M. Ferraris, *Storia dell'ontologia*, (Milan: Bompiani, 2008).

18 The importance of objects qua objects is the core of the so-called Object-Oriented Ontology (OOO), promoted especially by Graham Harman, Levi Bryant and Timothy Morton. For more on this, see the Afterword.

19 Immanuel Kant, *Critique of Pure Reason* (London: Penguin Classics, 2008) A 247/B 303.

20 M. Ferraris, 'Sum ergo cogito' in E.C. Corriero and A. Dezi (eds), *Realism and Nature in Schelling's Philosophy* (Turin: Accademia University Press, 2013d) and I.H. Grant 'What is an action? Ground and consequent in Schelling's philosophy of nature', in Emilio Carlo Corriero and Andrea Dezi (eds), *Realism and Nature in Schelling's*

Philosophy (Turin: Accademia University Press, 2013), pp. 187–201. See also Grant's *Philosophies of Nature after Schelling.*

21 See Ferraris, *Il Mondo esterno* (Milan: Bompiani, 2001b), new edition with foreword (Milano Bompiani, 2013).

22 M. Ferraris, *Ricostruire la decostruzione. Cinque saggi a partire da Jacques Derrida* (Milan: Bompiani, 2010b).

23 I refer the reader to M. Ferraris, *Filosofia globalizzata*, edited by Leonardo Caffo (Milan-Udine: Mimesis, 2013a).

24 Kant, *Critique of Pure Reason*, A51/B75.

25 E.B. Holt, W.T. Marvin, W.P. Montague, R.B. Perry, W.B. Pitkin and E.G. Spaulding, *The New Realism: Cooperative Studies in Philosophy* (New York: The Macmillan Company, 1912).

26 Arnaldo de Hollanda, *O Novo sistema Neo-Realista* (Ceara: Fortaleza, 1978).

27 For a more detailed analysis, see M. Ferraris, 'From postmodernism to realism', in Tiziana Andina (ed.), *Bridging the Analytic Continental Divide. A Companion to Contemporary Western Philosophy* (Boston, MA and Leiden: Brill, 2014d), pp. 1–7.

28 See John McDowell, *Mind and World* (Cambridge, MA: Harvard University Press, 1994).

29 In accordance with Michael Dummett, 'Realism' (1963), in M. Dummett, *Truth and Other Enigmas*, (Cambridge, MA: Harvard University Press, 1978), pp. 145–165.

Negativity

1 For more on this, see the chapter on 'Realitism' in M. Ferraris, *Manifesto of New Realism* (New York: SUNY Press, 2014e, forthcoming).

2 As Rorty posited: 'But none of us antirepresentationalists have ever doubted that most things in the universe are causally independent of us.

What we question is whether they are representationally independent of us'. Richard Rorty, 'Charles Taylor on truth', in R. Rorty, *Truth and Progress, Philosophical Papers*, vol. III (Cambridge: Cambridge University Press, 1998), p. 86. However, either 'representational dependence' involves some form of causal dependence, or it is hard to understand in what sense we can speak of 'dependence'.

3 Jean Baudrillard, *Art and Artefact* (London: SAGE), 1997.

4 'The aide said that guys like me were "in what we call the reality-based community," which he defined as people who "believe that solutions emerge from your judicious study of discernible reality." ... "That's not the way the world really works anymore," he continued. "We're an empire now, and when we act, we create our own reality. And while you're studying that reality—judiciously, as you will—we'll act again, creating other new realities, which you can study too, and that's how things will sort out. We're history's actors ... and you, all of you, will be left to just study what we do."'
Ron Suskind, 'Faith, certainty and the Presidency of George W. Bush', *The New York Times Magazine*, 17 October 2004, (reporting a statement by Karl Rove).

5 See Ferraris, *Manifesto of New Realism*.

6 R. Rorty, *Contingency, Irony, and Solidarity* (Cambridge: Cambridge University Press, 1989). For an analysis of the strategy of quotation marks see the remarkable article by Kevin Mulligan, 'How to destroy a European faculty of letters. Twenty five easy steps', in Göran Hermerén, Kerstin Sahlin and Nils-Eric Sahlin (eds), KVHAA Konferenser 81, *Trust and Confidence in Scientific Research* (Stockholm: Kungl. Vitterhetsakademien (KVHAA), the Royal Swedish Academy of Letters, History and Antiquities), pp. 23–36. I refer the reader back to Mulligan's text for a very interesting case study, some considerations of great insight, and an extensive bibliography.

7 Gilles Deleuze and Félix Guattari, *Anti-Oedipus: Capitalism and Schizophrenia* (Minneapolis, MN: University of Minnesota Press, 1983).

8 R. Rorty, *Solidarity or Objectivity?* (1984), in Michael Krausz (ed.), *Relativism: Interpretation and Confrontation* (Notre Dame, IN: University of Notre Dame Press, 1989), pp. 35–79.

9 I have no difficulty in saying that the social sciences or philosophy are not sciences without this meaning that they are myths or novels, as adherents of both scientism and hermeneutics posit – with a telling agreement.

10 This process had already begun between the nineteenth and the twentieth century. Dilthey wanted to found the *sciences* of the spirit, and planned to do so with psychology. Some objected that psychology is also a science of nature and, instead of answering 'so what?', he immediately changed his mind and turned to hermeneutics. In the same period, Husserl recommended *epoché* as regards existence so as not to interfere in the sciences, and Gentile asserted that we only have a relation with thought.

11 See Ferraris, *Manifesto of New Realism.*

12 Which can be located around the 1970s, with S. Kripke, *Naming and Necessity* (Cambridge, MA: Harvard University Press, 1980) and H. Putnam, 'The meaning of "meaning"', in H. Putnam, *Mind, Language and Reality. Philosophical Papers*, vol. 2, (Cambridge: Cambridge University Press, 1975), pp. 215–271.

13 And thus it can happen that something formally public actually turns out to be secret. For example, the documents relating to the sale of weapons in 115,000 gun shops in the United States are strictly on paper, precisely because (paradoxically) the bipartisan gun lobby wants to keep the secret at Congress. And it does so very banally by accumulating the receipts in a building not far from Washington, the National Tracing Center: thus, searching for the document (which is public and, in principle, not at all secret) will be like finding a needle in a haystack. Unless a future Assange decides to put them online.

14 Jürgen Habermas, 'Die Moderne/ein unvollendetes Projekt', in J. Habermas, *KleinePolitische Schriften* (Frankfurt /M.: Suhrkamp, 1981) pp. 444–464.

15 Paul Boghossian, *Fear of Knowledge Against Relativism and Constructivism* (New York: Oxford University Press, 2007).

16 David Rapport Lachterman, *The Ethics of Geometry: A Genealogy of Modernity* (London: Routledge, 1989). For a criticism of its contemporary outcomes, see also Boghossian, *Fear of Knowledge*. I believe that it is constructivism – rather than the 'correlationalism' questioned by Meillassoux (in *Après la finitude*) – that captures the main thread of modern philosophy, which does not simply lie in thinking about the object in *correlation* to the subject, but in conceiving of it as a result of a *construction* of the subject.

17 For a detailed analysis of the transcendental fallacy, see Ferraris, *Goodbye Kant!*.

18 René Descartes, *Discourse on Method and Metaphysical Meditations* (1641) (London and Felling on Tyne: The Walter Scott Publishing Co. Ltd, 1901).

19 David Hume, *A Treatise of Human Nature* (London: John Noon, 1739–40).

20 Kant, *Critique of Pure Reason*, A 1, B 1.

21 Georg Wilhelm Friedrich Hegel, *Phenomenology of Spirit* (New York: Oxford University Press, 2004).

22 'The time is out of joint: O cursed spite | That ever I was born to set it right!' (William Shakespeare, *Hamlet*, I.v.189–190).

23 Alfredo Ferrarin, 'Construction and mathematical schematism. Kant on the exhibition of a concept in intuition', *Kant-Studien* 86, 1995, pp. 131–174.

24 The first thinker to condemn the fallacy not in relation to Kant but to Hume was Thomas Reid, *Essays on the Active Powers of Man*, in Reid, *The Works of Thomas Reid, D.D.*, edited by Sir William Hamilton (Hildesheim: G. Olms Verlagsbuchhandlung, 1983 (first edition 1846)). His argument was resumed, this time also in reference to Kant, by Jacobi, who stated that when we relate to the world we do not make inferences starting from sense perception, nor do we ground them on the basis of categories. See Friedrich Heinrich Jacobi, *David Hume über den Glauben oder Idealismus und Realismus* (1787, 2nd re-elaborated edn 1815). Richard Avenarius (*Der menschliche Weltbegriff* (Leipzig: Reisland, 1891)) has the merit of providing a non-sceptical version of

Jacobi's criticism: the attempt to discover the conditions of possibility of experience systematically falsifies the character of experience, which is precisely that of immediacy.

25 Helmholtz rightly proposed to amend Kantian causality by giving it back to the physical world, for exactly the same reason for which, on the contrary, Schopenhauer proposed to give up all of Kantian categories, except causality. See Hermann von Helmholtz, 'The origin and meaning of geometrical axioms', *Mind* 3/10, 1878, pp. 212–225 (the quote is from pp. 223–224):

> Schopenhauer and many followers of Kant have been led to the improper conclusion that there is no real content at all in our space-perceptions, that space and its relations are purely transcendental and have nothing corresponding to them in the sphere of the real. We are, however, justified in taking our space-perceptions as signs of certain otherwise unknown relations in the world of reality, though we may not assume any sort of similarity between the sign and what is signified.

26 A very similar argument was developed by Meillassoux in his *Après la finitude*. Meillassoux spoke of 'ancestrality' and the 'arche-fossil' as a proof of the fact that there were things in the external world prior to any human existence. For more on this, see the Afterword.

27 Leading to 'correlationalism' (objects only exist in correlation to the subjects) criticised again by Meillassoux in *Après la finitude*.

28

> Berkeley in the beginning of the eighteenth century expressed very clearly the following concept. Reality is conceivable only in so far as the reality conceived is in relation to the activity which conceives it, and in that relation it is not only a possible object of knowledge, it is a present and actual one. To conceive reality is to conceive, at the same time and as one with it, the mind in which that reality is represented; and therefore the concept of a material reality is absurd.

Giovanni Gentile, *The Theory of Mind as a Pure Act* (London: Macmillan & Co., 1922).

29 See Ferraris, *Goodbye Kant!*

30 See Umberto Eco, Maurizio Ferraris and Diego Marconi, 'Lo schema del cane', *Rivista di estetica* 8, 1998, pp. 3–27.

31 H. Putnam, *Representation and Reality* (Cambridge, MA: MIT Press, 1988), p. 114.

32 See D. Marconi, 'Realismo minimale', in M. De Caro and M. Ferraris (eds), *Bentornata Realtà* (Turin: Einaudi, 2012), pp. 113–138.

Positivity

1 This theory was strongly rejected by Gibson's ecological perspective. See James Jerome Gibson, *The Ecological Approach to Visual Perception* (Boston, MA: Houghton Mifflin, 1979).

2 Thomas Kuhn, *The Structure of Scientific Revolutions* (Chicago, IL: University of Chicago Press, 1962).

3 M. Ferraris, 'Esistere è resistere', in M. De Caro and M. Ferraris (eds), *Bentornata realtà* (Turin: Einaudi, 2012b), pp. 139–165.

4 M. Ferraris, 'Causality and unamendableness', *Gestalt Theory*, 28/4, 2006a, pp. 401–407; M. Ferraris 'Reality as unamendability', in Luigi Cataldi Madonna (ed.), *Naturalistische Hermeneutik* (Würzburg: Königshausen & Neumann, 2013), pp. 113–129.

5 As regards unamendability, two clarifications are necessary. The first is that the reality cannot be corrected in the sense that things continue to exist regardless of what we think of them (while we can influence their existence through action, both in the social and in the physical world). Second, the notions of pre-existence, resistance, interaction and unamendability refer to a basic ontological factor: i.e. causality. The things of the world act causally (and so in a pre-existing, resistant, interactive and unamendable way) upon us, and we are in turn things in the world.

6 Gareth Evans, *The Varieties of Reference* (Oxford: Oxford University Press, 1984).

7 Karl Raimund Popper, *Logik der Forschung* (Vienna: Julius Springer, 1935).

8 See M. Ferraris, *Experimentelle Ästhetik* (Vienna: Turia und Kant, 2001a).

9 M. Ferraris, 'Metzger, Kant and the perception of causality', *The Dialogue. Yearbook of Philosophical Hermeneutics*, 1/2001c, pp. 126–134, and Ferraris 'Why perception matters', *Phenomenology and Mind*, 4, 2013e.

10 Paolo Bozzi, *Fisica ingenua. Oscillazioni, piani inclinati e altre storie: studi di psicologia della percezione* (Milan: Garzanti, 1990).

11 H. Putnam, 'Sense, nonsense and the senses. An inquiry into the powers of the human mind', *The Journal of Philosophy*, 91/9, 1994, pp. 445–517. Here Reid, James, Husserl, Wittgenstein and Austin are also related to naive realism.

12 I develop this topic in Maurizio Ferraris and Achille Varzi, 'Che cosa c'è e che cos'è', in VV.AA, *Nous* (Lecce: Milella, 2003), pp. 81–101 (see also Achille Varzi, *Il mondo messo a fuoco* (Roma-Bari: Laterza, 2010), pp. 5– 27). This can already be found in Strawson's programme of a 'descriptive metaphysics'; see Peter Strawson, *Individuals. An Essay in Descriptive Metaphysics* (Oxford: Oxford University Press,1959).

13 For a more detailed analysis of some of these moves, see Ferraris, *Documentality*.

14 Nelson Goodman, *Ways of Worldmaking* (Indianapolis, IN: Hackett, 1978).

15 H. Putnam, *The Many Faces of Realism* (LaSalle, IL: Open Court, 1987a), chapters 1, 2; and H. Putnam, 'Truth and convention: on Davidson's refutation of conceptual relativism', *Dialectica* 41, 1987b, pp. 69–77 (reprinted in Putnam, *Realism with a Human Face* (Cambridge, MA: Harvard University Press, 1990) pp. 96–104).

16 Willard Van Orman Quine, 'Designation and existence', *Journal of Philosophy*, 36/26, 1939, pp. 701–709. See p. 708:

> Here then are five ways of saying the same thing: 'There is such a thing as appendicitis'; 'The word "appendicitis" designates'; 'The word

"appendicitis" is a name'; 'The word "appendicitis" is a substituted for a variable'; 'The disease appendicitis is a value of a variable'. The universe of entities is the range of values of variables. To be is to be the value of a variable.

17 The ω-reality is what Lacan referred to by saying that hallucinations are pure real, as not compromised with the symbolic; that is to say, the real with its autonomy and its structure, long before the subject's entrance into it. See Jacques Lacan, *Le Sèminaire. Livre III. Les psychoses* (1955–1956) (Paris: Seuil, 1981). English translation: *The Psychoses, The Seminars of Jacques Lacan*, edited by Jacques-Alain Miller, Book III 1955–1956 (London: Routledge, 1993).

18 Following a path that starts with Aristotle's *Metaphysics* and passes through Meinong's *Theory of the Object,* up until contemporary 'object-oriented philosophy': see G. Harman, *Guerrilla Metaphysics. Phenomenology and the Carpentry of Things* (Chicago, IL: Open Court, 2005) and Harman, *The Quadruple Object*; Roy Bhaskar, *A Realist Theory of Science* (London: Routledge, 2008); Levi Bryant, *The Democracy of Objects* (Ann Arbor, MI: Open Humanities Press, 2011); and, on a different path, Tristan Garcia, *Forme et objet* (Paris: Presses Universitaires de France, 2011).

19 For an in-depth discussion of this scheme, see Ferraris, *Documentality.*

20 Ferraris, *Il mondo esterno*, pp. 90–91. I present this argument through the 'slipper experiment', now available in English in Ferraris, *Documentality* and in Ferraris, *Manifesto of New Realism*.

21 Thomas Nagel, 'What is it like to be a bat?' *Philosophical Review* 83/4, 1974, pp. 435–450.

22 For instance, Quentin Meillassoux and Graham Harman. For a deeper analysis, see the Afterword.

23 See note 73.

24 Kripke, *Naming and Necessity*.

25 As put by Manuel de Landa, 'the world is filled with objective tendencies and capacities waiting to be actualized by skillful interventions, tendencies and capacities that provide a myriad of opportunities and risks' (Manuel de Landa, 'Ontological conmitments', *Speculations, A Journal of Speculative Realism* IV, 2013, p. 73). By using the term 'affordance' I am referring to a notion that has been widely popular during the last century: see Gibson, *The Ecological Approach to Visual Perception*; Kurt Lewin, 'Untersuchungen zur Handlungs- und Affekt-Psychologie. I. Vorbemerkung über die psychischen Kräfte und Energien und über die Struktur der Seele', *Psychologische Forschung* 7, 1926, pp. 294–329. Fichte had already spoken of an 'Aufforderungskaracter' of the real, see Johann Gottlieb Fichte, *Grundlage des Naturrechts* ('Zweiter Lehrsatz') (1796), ch. 1, § 3, Gesamtausgabe der bayerischen Akademie der Wissenschften, Stuttgart-Bad Cannstatt: Frommann-Holzboog, vol. I/3, pp. 342–351.

26 Umberto Eco, *Interpretation and Overinterpretation* (Cambridge: Cambridge University Press, 1992).

27 H. Putnam, 'Brains in a vat', H. Putnam, *Reason, Truth, and History* (Cambridge, MA: Cambridge University Press, 1981a), pp. 1–22.

28 As I mentioned earlier, positive realism dates back to the later Schelling and his claim that 'it is not because there is thinking that there is being, but rather the converse: it is because there is being that there is thinking' (Friedrich Wilhelm Joseph Schelling, *Grounding of Positive Philosophy* (New York: SUNY University Press, 2007), p. 203). This was noted by Grant in *Philosophies of Nature After Schelling.*

Normativity

1 This section is based on an article by Prof. Ferraris that appeared on the Monist: http://www.pdcnet.org/pdc/bvdb.nsf/purchase?openform&fp=monist&id=monist_2014_0097_0002_0200_0221

2 Marshall McLuhan, *Understanding Media. The Extentions of Man* (New York: McGraw Hill, 1964).

3 Ferraris, *Where are you?* See also Ferraris, 'Where are you? Mobile ontology', in Kristof Nyíri (ed.), *Mobile Understanding. The Epistemology of Ubiquitous Communication* (Vienna: Passagen Verlag, 2006b), pp. 41–52.

4 Bauman's, from this point of view, is an institutionalisation and perennialisation of postmodernism. Even though not one of his theses proved to be empirically founded (see Zygmunt Bauman, *Liquid Modernity* (Cambridge: Polity Press, 2000)).

5 Apart from the already mentioned *Documentality*, I refer the reader back to M. Ferraris, 'Documentality, or, why nothing social exists beyond the text', in Christian Kanzian and Edmund Runggaldier (eds), *Cultures. Conflict – Analysis – Dialogue, Proceedings of the 29th International Ludwig Wittgenstein-Symposium in Kirchberg, Austria*, Publications of the Austrian Ludwig Wittgenstein Society (Berlin: Walter de Gruyter & Co.), New Series 3, 2007c, pp. 385–401; M. Ferraris, 'Documentality, or Europe', *The Monist*, 92/2, 2009, pp. 286–314 and M. Ferraris, 'Social ontology and documentality', in Riccardo Pozzo and Marco Sgarbi (eds), *Eine Typologie der Formen der Begriffsgeschichte*, Archiv für Begriffsgeschichte, Sonderheft 7 (Jg. 2010a), pp. 133–148. An important development of documentality was provided by Barry Smith, 'Document Acts', *Proceedings of the Conference on Collective Intentionality*, Basel, Switzerland, 23–26 August, 2010.

6 In this sense, writing makes social objects structurally similar to living entities. This is why, in *Documentality*, I refer to the parallelism offered by Richard Dawkins in *The Selfish Gene* (Oxford: Oxford University Press, 1976) between genes and 'memes'.

7 See M. Ferraris, *Anima e iPad* (Parma: Guanda 2011).

8 It should be noted that this principle applies also to the production of a very peculiar type of social object: the work of art. The artwork is the result of an act involving at least one author and a recipient (even someone who writes only 'for themselves' postulates an audience of some kind). Artworks are specific types of documents, i.e. inscriptions that record social acts. See M. Ferraris, *La fidanzata automatica* (Milan: Bompiani, 2007a) – the thesis expressed in this book partially appears in *Where Are You? An Ontology of the Cell Phone*.

9 Ludwig Wittgenstein, *Philosophical Investigations* (Oxford: Basil Blackwell Ltd, 1953), §§243 and ff.

10 I tried to analyse this philosophical mythology in M. Ferraris, *La filosofia e lo spirito vivente* (Roma-Bari: Laterza, 1991).

11 For instance, in the film *The King's Speech* (United Kingdom, 2010), the speech that George VI gave in 1939 was written by others, and – since the king was a stutterer – it was also long rehearsed with a speech therapist. And yet, who would doubt that the speech is actually the king's?

12 I analysed the process by which the original is the result of imitation in M. Ferraris, *Mimica. Lutto e autobiografia da Agostino a Heidegger* (Milan: Bompiani, 1992).

13 'It is, for example, a mistake to treat money and other such instruments as if they were natural phenomena like the phenomena studied in physics, chemistry, and biology. The recent economic crisis makes it clear that they are products of massive fantasy.' John Searle, *Making the Social World: The Structure of Human Civilization* (New York: Oxford University Press, 2010), p. 201.

14 Margaret Gilbert, 'Walking together: a paradigmatic social phenomenon', *Midwest Studies In Philosophy* 15, 1990, pp. 1–14.

15 An important reference here is the theory of 'games of make-believe' proposed in Walton: Kendall Walton, *Mimesis as Make-believe: On the Foundations of the Representational Arts* (Cambridge, MA: Harvard University Press, 1990), which Amie Thomasson compares with Searle's social ontology: Amie Thomasson, 'Foundations for a social ontology', *Proto-Sociology: An International Journal of Interdisciplinary Resarch and Project* 18–19, 2003, pp. 269–290.

16 Searle, 'The campus war: a sympathetic look at the university in agony', 1971, http://www.ditext.com/searle/campus/campus.html [Accessed 4 April 2014].

17 In agreement with the argument against private language proposed by Wittgenstein (see note 97), there must be at least two people not only to produce a document, but also to have a language and, more generally, a rule.

18 See François Recanati, *Mental Files* (Oxford: Oxford University Press, 2012).

19 Robert Brandom, *Making it Explicit: Reasoning, Representing, and Discursive Commitment* (Cambridge, MA: Harvard University Press, 1994), chapter 1.

20 For a more detailed articulation of these two fundamental theses, see Ferraris, *Anima e iPad*.

21 Concretely, let us take the uninterrupted stream of texts (20 billion documents) that is the Web, see the exchanges between people and, starting from use, derive the meaning. On this basis Comprendo has developed a system of automatic Italian-English translation, and in Pisa the system Piqasso (Pisa Question Answering System) was developed, able to automatically extract answers from the Web (a similar system developed by IBM managed to beat the competitors at a popular American quiz game).

22 Bert Hölldobler and Edward Osborne Wilson, *The Superorganism: The Beauty, Elegance, and Strangeness of Insect Societies* (New York: W.W. Norton & Co., 2008).

23 See Daniel Clement Dennett, 'Darwin's "strange inversion of reasoning"', *Proceedings of the National Academy of Sciences of the United States of America* 106 Suppl. 1, 2009, pp. 10061–10065.

24 Pierre Lévy, *L'Intelligence collective. Pour une anthropologie du cyberespace* (Paris: La Découverte, 1994).

25 M. Ferraris, 'Community', *La Repubblica*, 14 July 2010c.

26 Friedrich Kittler, *Gramophone Film Typewriter* (Stanford, CA: Stanford University Press, 1999). The German original dates back to 1986.

27 As is suggested by Kevin Kelly, *What Technology Wants* (New York: Viking Press, 2010). Nevertheless, it is an old idea that goes from Spengler to Jünger and Heidegger.

28 This is extensively developed in Ferraris, *Anima e iPad*.

29 Well clarified by Roberto Casati in *Contro il colonialismo digitale* (Rome-Bari: Laterza, 2013). See also M. Ferraris, *Sans Papier* (Rome: Castelvecchi, 2007b).

30 Another thing that is likely to resemble fast-thought of the web is that idling discourse, disconnected both from the truth and from the lie, described by Harry Frankfurt in *On Bullshit* (Princeton, NJ: Princeton University Press, 1986).

31 Pierre Bourdieu, *On Television* (New York: The New Press, 1998). I have developed this argument in M. Ferraris 'Quando il pensare veloce aumenta la petulanza', *La Repubblica*, 4 August 2013f.

32 Thus, the digital relationships mentioned by Antonio Casilli in *Les liaisons numériques* (Paris: Seuil, 2011) are undoubtedly *Liaisons dangereuses*, dangerous relationships. After all, the novel by Laclos is a proto-chat, in which the correspondence between Valmont and Madame de Merteuil is destined to cause the misfortune of other victims, sacrificed to the cruel vanity of the two main correspondents. It is said that the Web feeds narcissism, which is very likely, but it is a double-edged sword, since it can also be the source of great disappointments. Above all, more than an area of reward and recognition – the harmonious unfolding of collective intelligence and universal love which (with an incurable optimism) people fantasised about when the Internet took its first steps – the space of the Web is a battlefield, a polemic and political sphere.

33 Friedrich Nietzsche, *On The Genealogy of Morals* (New York: Courier Dover Publications, 2003), p. 34. On this acknowledgement of the specifically human ability to make promises (and, more generally, commitments and entitlements) I refer the reader again to the first chapter of *Making it Explicit* by Brandom, who in turn refers to Kant's idea that humans are essentially 'distinctively normative, or rule-governed, creatures' (Brandom 1994, p. 9).

Afterword

1 One of the main philosophers who favoured hermeneutics and solidarity over objectivity and truth is Richard Rorty, whose *Philosophy and the Mirror of Nature* (Princeton, NJ: Princeton University Press, 1979) is considered one of the seminal texts of postmodern philosophy.

2 Graham Harman, 'The current state of speculative realism', *Speculations* IV, 2013, p. 23: 2002 was the publication year of Harman's *Tool-being: Heidegger and the Metaphysics of Objects* (Chicago, IL: Open Court, 2002) and Manuel De Landa's *Intensive Science and Virtual Philosophy* (London: Continuum, 2002).

3 Maurizio Ferraris, 'Esistere è resistere', in Mario De Caro and Maurizio Ferraris (eds), *Bentornata Realtà* (Turin: Einaudi, 2012), pp. 139–167.

4 Donald Davidson, *Inquiries into Truth and Interpretation* (Oxford: Oxford University Press, 1984).

5 Nelson Goodman, *Ways of Worldmaking* (Indianapolis, IN: Hackett, 1978).

6 Quentin Meillassoux, http://www.urbanomic.com/Documents/Documents-1.pdf, 22 July 2010, p. 10 [Accessed 2 April 2014].

7 Ferraris often refers to his own position as being similar to Umberto Eco's as it is expressed in Eco's *Interpretation and Overinterpretation* (Cambridge: Cambridge University Press, 1992).

8 Various new realisms were discussed at a recent conference: 'Fridericianum Symposium Speculations on Anonymous Materials' (Kassel, 4 January 2014).

9 Harman, 'The current state of speculative realism', p. 22.

10 For a full review of the debate around Italian New Realism, see http://nuovorealismo.wordpress.com. To give just one significant example regarding speculative realism, the publisher and arts organisation Urbanomic commissioned the sound artist Florian Hecker to make a new work exploring the themes addressed in Meillassoux's book *After Finitude*. This collaboration resulted in the release of *Speculative Solution*, a CD and book with contributions by Florian Hecker, Elie Ayache, Robin Mackay and Quentin Meillassoux. This collaborative project brings together Hecker's sonic practice and psychoacoustic experimentation and Meillassoux's concept of 'hyperchaos' – the absolute contingency of the laws of nature.

11 Iain Hamilton Grant, *Philosophies of Nature After Schelling* (London: Continuum, 2006).

12 Ray Brassier, *Nihil Unbound. Enlightenment and Extinction* (London: Pallgrave Macmillan, 2007).

13 According to Harman, the four original speculative realists can be divided on the basis of their epistemism: this places Harman and Grant on one side, and Meillassoux and Brassier on the other. (See Harman, 'The current state of speculative realism', pp. 23–27). By choosing to focus on Harman and Meillassoux, we will hopefully give the reader an idea of both 'kinds' of speculative realism.

14 Levi Bryant, *The Democracy of Objects* (Ann Arbor, MI: Open Humanities Press, 2011).

15 See, for example, G. Harman, *The Quadruple Object* (London: Zer0 Books, 2011), and M. Ferraris, *Manifesto of New Realism* (New York: SUNY Press, 2014).

16 G. Harman, 'The road to objects', *continent*, 1.3, 2011, pp. 171–179.

17 While for Meillassoux's speculative materialism it is precisely the other way round.

18 This is more extensively addressed in Harman's *Tool-being*.

19 Harman, *The Quadruple Object*, p. 46.

20 M. Ferraris, *Goodbye Kant! What Still Stands of the Critique of Pure Reason* (New York: SUNY Press, 2013b).

21 Q. Meillassoux, *After Finitude* (London: Continuum, 2008), p. 5.

22 Q. Meillassoux, http://www.urbanomic.com/Documents/Documents-1.pdf, p. 10.

23 Meillassoux, *After Finitude*, p. 27.

24 Robin Mackay, http://www.urbanomic.com/Documents/Documents-1.pdf, 22 July 2010, p. 9 [Accessed 2 April 2014].

25 Wilfrid S. Sellars was the first to distinguish between 'manifest image' and 'scientific image', the latter being the discourse of science (quanta, subatomic particles and so on). The former is defined as: 'the framework in terms of which man came to be aware of himself as man-in-the-world' (Wilfrid S. Sellars, *Science, Perception and Reality*, London: Routledge &

Kegan Paul Ltd and New York: The Humanities Press, 1963, p. 6). More broadly, it is the framework through which we ordinarily observe and explain our world. The manifest image is seen as prior to the scientific image.

26 Ferraris' early commitment to realism was noted by Harman in his preface to Ferraris' *Manifesto of New Realism*.

27 Alexander Gottlieb Baumgarten, *Aesthetica/Ästhetik* (1750), edited by Dagmar Mirbach, 2 vol. (Hamburg: Felix Meiner Verlag, 2007).

28 This topic later reappeared in the *Manifesto of New Realism*, where a whole section is dedicated to the return to a 'New Enlightenment'.

29 M. Ferraris, *Estetica razionale* (Milan: Raffaello Cortina, 1997), p. 69, our translation.

30 Ferraris, *Estetica razionale*, p. 49, our translation.

31 Ferraris, *Estetica razionale*, pp. 69–70, our translation.

32 M. Ferraris, 'Why perception matters', *Phenomenology and Mind* 4, 2013c, 55–56.

33 Ferraris, 'Why perception matters', p. 56.

34 M. Ferraris, 'Sum ergo cogito', in Emilio Carlo Corriero and Andrea Dezi (eds), *Nature and Realism in Schelling's Philosophy* (Turin: Accademia University Press, 2013a), pp. 187–201. For more on Schelling's influence over contemporary realism, see Grant, *Philosophies of Nature After Schelling*.

35 Rorty, *Philosophy and the Mirror of Nature*, p. 178.

36 Paolo Bozzi, *Fisica ingenua. Oscillazioni, piani inclinati e altre storie: studi di psicologia della percezione* (Milan: Garzanti, 1990).

37 Ferraris, 'Why perception matters', p. 57.

38 It is worth noting that as early as 1994 Putnam proposed a return to Aristotle's *De anima*. See the chapters 'The Return of Aristotle', 'Changing Aristotle's Mind', 'Aristotle after Wittgenstein', in H. Putnam, *Words and Life*, edited by James Conant (Cambridge: Cambridge University Press, 1994).

39 H. Putnam, *The Threefold Cord: Mind, Body, and the World* (New York: Columbia University Press, 1999), p. 11.

40 H. Putnam, 'Realismo sì o no? Sbagliava anche Russell', *La Stampa*, 4 December 2012b, our translation.

41 Very briefly, Gabriel's theory stems from the argument from facticity: namely, if we agree that, at least, 'there is something', then there is at least one absolute fact, that is true anyway, namely *the fact that there is something*. He then combines this with ontological realism, according to which to exist is to belong to a certain domain. The world has a complicated structure, so you should not link ontology with metaphysics, trying to find the underlying structure of the universe. He advocates plurivocity, while maintaining that we can talk about how things really are. Only, they are not in one single way.

42 H. Putnam, 'On not writing off scientific realism', in H. Putnam, *Philosophy in an Age of Science* (Cambridge, MA: Harvard University Press, 2012), pp. 91–108.

43 Ferraris, *Manifesto of New Realism*.

44 H. Putnam, 'Realismo e senso comune', in M. De Caro and M. Ferraris (eds), *Bentornata realtà* (Turin: Einaudi), p. 15.

45 Indeed, speculative realists reject common sense altogether. Graham Harman has spoken about H. P. Lovecratft as 'a sort of mascot for the "speculative" part of speculative realism, since his grotesque semi-Euclidean monsters symbolise the rejection of everyday common sense to which speculative realism aspires.' See G. Harman, 'The road to objects,' p. 171.

46 Timothy Morton, 'Objects as temporary autonomous zones', *continent.*, 1.3, 2011, p. 150.

47 Timothy Morton, *Realist Magic: Objects, Ontology, Causality* (Ann Arbor, MI: Open Humanity Press, 2013), p. 222.

48 Morton, *Realist Magic*, p. 222.

49 Harman, *The Quadruple Object*, p. 20.

50 Harman, *The Quadruple Object*, p. 44.

51 Harman, *The Quadruple Object*, p. 72.

52 Meillassoux, *After Finitude*, p. 27.

53 Meillassoux, *After Finitude*, p. 32.

54 Meillassoux, *After Finitude*, p. 57.

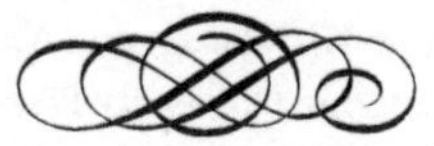

Bibliography

Andina, T. (ed), *Bridging the Analytic Continental Divide. A Companion to Contemporary Western Philosophy*, Boston, MA and Leiden: Brill, 2014.

Avenarius, R., *Der menschliche Weltbegriff*, Leipzig: Reisland, 1891.

Baudrillard, J., *Art and Artefact*, London: SAGE, 1997.

Bauman, Z., *Liquid Modernity*, Cambridge: Polity Press, 2000.

Benoist, J., 'Reality', *Meta: Research in Hermeneutics, Phenomenology and Practical Philosophy*, Special Issue on New Realism, 2014, pp. 21–27.

Beuchot, M. and Jerez, J.L., *Manifiesto del Nuevo Realismo Analógico*, Buenos Aires: Editorial Círculo Erméneutico, 2013.

Bhaskar, R., *A Realist Theory of Science*, London: Routledge, 2008.

Boghossian, P., *Fear of knowledge Against Relativism and Constructivism*, New York: Oxford University Press, 2007.

Bozzi, P., *Fisica ingenua*, Milan: Garzanti, 1990.

Bourdieu, P., *On Television*, New York: The New Press, 1998.

Brandom, R., *Making it Explicit: Reasoning, Representing, and Discursive Commitment*, Cambridge, MA: Harvard University Press, 1994.

Brassier, R., *Nihil Unbound. Enlightenment and Extinction*, London: Palgrave Macmillan, 2007.

Bryant, L.R., *The Democracy of Objects*, Ann Arbor, MI: Open Humanities Press, 2011.

Bryant, L.R., Harman, G. and Srnicek, N. (eds), *The Speculative Turn. Continental Materialism and Realism*, Melbourne: re.press, 2011.

Casati, R., *Contro il colonialismo digitale*, Roma-Bari: Laterza, 2013.

Casilli, A., *Les liaisons numériques*, Paris: Seuil, 2011.

Corriero, E.C. and Dezi, A. (eds), *Realism and Nature in Schelling's Philosophy*, Turin: Accademia University Press, 2013.

Dakwins, R., *The Selfish Gene*, Oxford: Oxford University Press, 1976.

De Caro, M., 'Il lungo viaggio di Hilary Putnam. Realismo metafisico, antirealismo e realismo naturale', *Lingua e stile* 4, 1996, pp. 527–545.

De Caro, M. and Ferraris, M. (eds), *Bentornata Realtà*, Turin: Einaudi, 2012.

de Hollanda, A., *O Novo sistema Neo-Realista*, Fortaleza: Ceara, 1978.

de Landa, M., 'Ontological conmitments', *Speculations: A Journal of Speculative Realism*, IV, 2013, pp. 71–73.

Deleuze, G. and Guattari, F., *Anti-Oedipus: Capitalism and Schizophrenia*, Minneapolis, MN: University of Minnesota Press, 1983.

Dennett, D.C., 'Darwin's "strange inversion of reasoning"', *Proceedings of the National Academy of Sciences of the United States of America* 106 Suppl. 1, 2009, pp. 10061–10065.

Derrida, J., *Margins of Philosophy*, Brighton: Harvester Press, 1982.

Derrida, J. and Ferraris, M., *A Taste for the Secret*, Ithaca, NY and London: Cornell University Press, 2001.

Descartes, R., *Discourse on Method and Metaphysical Meditations* (1641), London and Felling-On-Tyne: The Walter Scott Publishing Co. Ltd, 1901.

Dummett, M., 'Realism' (1963), in Dummett, M., *Truth and Other Enigmas*, Cambridge, MA: Harvard University Press, 1978, pp. 145–165.

Dummett, M., *Truth and Other Enigmas*, Cambridge, MA: Harvard University Press, 1978.

Eco, U., *The Limits of Interpretation*, Bloomington, IN: Indiana University Press, 1990.

Eco, U., *Interpretation and Overinterpretation*, Cambridge: Cambridge University Press, 1992.

Eco, U., *Kant and the Platypus: Essays on Language and Cognition*, Boston, MA: Houghton Mifflin Harcourt, 1999.

Eco, U., Ferraris, M. and Marconi, D., 'Lo schema del cane', *Rivista di estetica*, 8, 1998, pp. 3–27.

Evans, G., *The Varieties of Reference*, Oxford: Oxford University Press, 1984.

Ferrarin, A., 'Construction and mathematical schematism. Kant on the exhibition of a concept in intuition', *Kant-Studien* 86, 1995, pp. 131–174.

Ferraris, M., *La filosofia e lo spirito vivente*, Roma-Bari: Laterza, 1991.
Ferraris, M., *Mimica. Lutto e autobiografia da Agostino a Heidegger*, Milan: Bompiani, 1992.
Ferraris, M., *Estetica razionale*, Milan: Raffaello Cortina, 1997.
Ferraris, M., *Experimentelle Ästhetik*, Vienna: Turia und Kant, 2001a.
Ferraris, M., *Il Mondo esterno*, Milan: Bompiani, 2001b.
Ferraris, M., 'Metzger, Kant and the perception of causality', *The Dialogue. Yearbook of Philosophical Hermeneutics* 1, 2001c, pp. 126–134.
Ferraris, M., 'Causality and unamendableness', *Gestalt Theory* 28/4, 2006a, pp. 401–407.
Ferraris, M., 'Where are you? Mobile ontology', in K. Nyíri (ed.), *Mobile Understanding. The Epistemology of Ubiquitous Communication*, Vienna: Passagen, 2006b, pp. 41–52.
Ferraris, M., *La Fidanzata Automatica*, Milan: Bompiani, 2007a.
Ferraris, M., *Sans Papier*, Rome: Castelvecchi, 2007b.
Ferraris, M., 'Documentality, or, why nothing social exists beyond the text', in C. Kanzian and E. Runggaldier (eds), *Cultures. Conflict – Analysis – Dialogue, Proceedings of the 29th International Ludwig Wittgenstein-Symposium in Kirchberg, Austria*, Publications of the Austrian Ludwig Wittgenstein Society, Berlin: Walter de Gruyter, New Series 3, 2007c, pp. 385–401.
Ferraris, M., *Storia dell'ontologia*, Milan: Bompiani, 2008.
Ferraris, M., 'Documentality, or Europe', *The Monist* 92/2, 2009, pp. 286–314.
Ferraris, M., 'Social ontology and documentality', in R. Pozzo, and M. Sgarbi (eds), *Eine Typologie der Formen der Begriffsgeschichte*, Archiv für Begriffsgeschichte, Sonderheft 7, 2010a, pp. 133–148.
Ferraris, M., *Ricostruire la decostruzione. Cinque saggi a partire da Jacques Derrida*, Milan: Bompiani, 2010b.
Ferraris, M., 'Community', *La Repubblica*, 14 July 2010c.
Ferraris, M., *Anima e iPad*, Parma: Guanda, 2011a.
Ferraris, M., 'Nuovo Realismo', *Rivista di estetica* 48/3, 2011b, pp. 69–93.
Ferraris, M., *Documentality. Why It Is Necessary to Leave Traces*, New York: Fordham University Press, 2012a.
Ferraris, M., 'Esistere è resistere', in M. De Caro and M. Ferraris (eds), *Bentornata realtà*, Turin: Einaudi, 2012b, pp. 139–166.
Ferraris, M., 'The aging of the "school of suspicion"', in G. Vattimo and P. A. Rovatti (eds), *Weak Thought*, New York: SUNY Press, 2012c.

Ferraris, M., *Manifesto del nuovo realismo*, Laterza: Roma-Bari, 2012d.

Ferraris, M., *Filosofia globalizzata*, edited by L. Caffo, Milan-Udine: Mimesis, 2013a.

Ferraris, M., *Goodbye Kant! What Still Stands of the Critique of Pure Reason*, New York: SUNY Press, 2013b.

Ferraris, M., 'Reality as unamendability', in L. Cataldi Madonna (ed.), *Naturalistische Hermeneutik*, Wuerzburg: Königshausen u. Neumann, 2013c, pp. 113–129.

Ferraris, M., 'Sum ergo cogito', in E.C. Corriero and A. Dezi (eds), *Realism and Nature in Schelling's Philosophy*, Turin: Accademia University Press, 2013d, pp. 187–201.

Ferraris, M., 'Why perception matters', *Phenomenology and Mind* 4, 2013e. http://www.phenomenologyandmind.eu/wp-content/uploads/2013/07/M.Ferraris.pdf [accessed 4 April 2014].

Ferraris, M., 'Quando il pensare veloce aumenta la petulanza', *La Repubblica*, 4 August 2013f.

Ferraris, M., 'New realism as positive realism', *Meta: Research in Hermeneutics, Phenomenology and Practical Philosophy*, Special Issue on New Realism, 2014a, pp. 172–213.

Ferraris, M., *Manifesto of New Realism*, New York: SUNY Press, 2014b.

Ferraris, M., *Where Are You? An Ontology of the Cell Phone*, New York: Fordham University Press, 2014c.

Ferraris, M., 'From Postmodernism to Realism', in Tiziana Andina (ed.), *Bridging the Analytic Continental Divide. A Companion to Contemporary Western Philosophy*, Boston, MA and Leiden: Brill, 2014d), pp. 1–7.

Ferraris, M., 'Realitism', in M. Ferraris, *Manifesto of New Realism*, New York: SUNY Press, 2014e, forthcoming.

Ferraris, M. and Varzi, A., 'Che cosa c'è e che cos'è', in *Nous*, Lecce: Milella, 2003, pp. 81–101.

Fichte, J.G., *Grundlage des Naturrechts* ('Zweiter Lehrsatz'), ch. 1, § 3, Gesamtausgabe der bayerischen Akademie der Wissenschften, Stuttgart-Bad Cannstatt, Frommann-Holzboog, I/3, 1796, pp. 342–351.

Frankfurt, Harry., *On Bullshit*, Princeton, NJ: Princeton University Press, 1986.

Gabriel, M., *Warum es die Welt nicht gibt*, Berlin: Ullstein, 2013.

Gabriel, M., *Fields of Sense. A New Realist Ontology*, Edinburgh: Edinburgh University Press, 2014.

Gabriel, M., 'Is Heidegger's "turn" a realist project?', *Meta: Research in Hermeneutics, Phenomenology and Practical Philosophy*, Special Issue on New Realism, 2014, pp. 44–73.

Garcia, T. *Forme et objet*, Paris: Presses Universitaires de France, 2011.

Gentile, G., *The theory of Mind as a Pure Act*, London: Macmillan & Co, 1922.

Gilbert, M., 'Walking together: a paradigmatic social phenomenon', *Midwest Studies In Philosophy* 15, 1990, pp. 1–14.

Gibson, J.J. *The Ecological Approach to Visual Perception*, Boston, MA: Houghton Mifflin, 1979.

Goodman, N., *Ways of Worldmaking*, Indianapolis, IN: Hackett, 1978.

Grant, I.H., *Philosophies of Nature after Schelling*, New York-London: Continuum, 2006.

Grant, I.H. 'What is an action? Ground and consequence in Schelling's philosophy of nature', in Emilio Carlo Corriero and Andrea Dezi (eds), *Realism and Nature in Schelling's Philosophy*, Turin: Accademia University Press, 2013.

Habermas, J., 'Die Moderne/ein unvollendetes Projekt', *KleinePolitische Schriften*, Frankfurt/M.: Suhrkamp, 1981, pp. 444–464.

Harman, G., *Guerrilla Metaphysics. Phenomenology and the Carpentry of Things*, Chicago, IL: Open Court, 2005.

Harman, G., *The Quadruple Object*, London: Zer0 Books, 2011.

Harman, G., 'The current state of speculative realism', *Speculations: A Journal of Speculative Realism*, IV, 2013, pp. 22–28.

Hegel, G.W.F., *Phenomenology of Spirit*, New York: Oxford University Press, 2004.

Helmholtz, W. 'The origin and meaning of geometrical axioms', *Mind* 3/10, 1878, pp. 212–225.

Hölldobler, B. and Wilson, E.O., *The Superorganism: The Beauty, Elegance, and Strangeness of Insect Societies*, New York: W.W. Norton & Co., 2008.

Holt, E.B., Marvin, W.T., Montague, W.P., Perry, R.B., Pitkin, W.B. and Spaulding E.G., *The New Realism: Cooperative Studies in Philosophy*, New York: The Macmillan Company, 1912.

Hume, D., *A Treatise of Human Nature*, London: John Noon, 1739–40.

Jacobi, F.H., *David Hume über den Glauben oder Idealismus und Realismus*, Breslau: G. Loeve, 1787 (2nd re-elaborated edn 1815).

Kant, I., *The Critique of Pure Reason*, London: Penguin Classics, 2008.

Kelly, K., *What Technology Wants*, New York: Viking Press, York 2010.

Kittler, F., *Gramophone Film Typewriter*, Stanford, CA: Stanford University Press, 1999.

Kripke, S., *Naming and Necessity*, Cambridge, MA: Harvard University Press, 1980.

Kuhn, Th., *The Structure of Scientific Revolutions*, Chicago, IL: University of Chicago Press, 1962.

Lacan, J., *Le Sèminaire. Livre III. Les psychoses (1955–1956)*, Paris: Seuil, 1981. English translation: *The Psychoses, The Seminars of Jacques Lacan*, edited by Jacques-Alain Miller, Book III 1955–1956, London: Routledge, 1993.

Lachterman, D.R., *The Ethics of Geometry: A Genealogy of Modernity*, London: Routledge, 1989.

Lévy, P., *L'Intelligence collective. Pour une anthropologie du cyberespace*, Paris: La Découverte, 1994.

Lewin, K., 'Untersuchungen zur Handlungs- und Affekt-Psychologie. I. Vorbemerkung über die psychischen Kräfte und Energien und über die Struktur der Seele', *Psychologische Forschung* 7, 1926, pp. 294–329.

Marconi, D., 'Realismo minimale', in M. De Caro and M. Ferraris (eds), *Bentornata Realtà*, Turin: Einaudi, 2012, pp. 113–138.

McDowell, J., *Mind and World*, Cambridge, MA: Harvard University Press, 1994.

McLuhan, M., *Understanding Media. The Extentions of Man*, New York: McGraw Hill, 1964.

Meillassoux, Q., *Après la finitude. Essai sur la nécessité de la contingence*, Paris: Seuil, 2006.

Mulligan, K., 'How to destroy a European faculty of letters. Twenty five easy steps', *KVHAA Konferenser* 81, *Trust and Confidence in Scientific Research*, edited by G. Hermerén, K. Sahlin and N-E. Sahlin, Kungl. Vitterhetsakademien (KVHAA), the Royal Swedish Academy of Letters, History and Antiquities, Stockholm, pp. 23–36.

Nagel, Th., 'What is it like to be a bat?', *Philosophical Review* 83/4, 1974, pp. 435–450.

Nietzsche, F., *On The Genealogy of Morals*, New York: Courier Dover Publications, 2003.

Popper, K.R., *Logik der Forschung*, Vienna: Julius Springer, 1935.

Putnam, H., 'The meaning of "meaning"', in *Mind, Language and Reality. Philosophical Papers*, vol. 2., Cambridge: Cambridge University Press, 1975, pp. 215–271.

Putnam, H., *Mind, Language and Reality. Philosophical Papers*, vol. 2., Cambridge: Cambridge University Press, 1975.

Putnam, H., *Meaning and the Moral Sciences*, London: Routledge and Kegan Paul, 1978.

Putnam, H., 'Brains in a vat', in *Reason, Truth, and History*, Cambridge: Cambridge University Press, 1981a, pp. 1–22.

Putnam, H., *Reason, Truth, and History*, Cambridge: Cambridge University Press, 1981b.

Putnam, H., *The Many Faces of Realism*, LaSalle, IL: Open Court, 1987.

Putnam, 'Truth and convention: on Davidson's refutation of conceptual relativism', *Dialectica* 41, 1987, pp. 69–77.

Putnam, H., *Representation and Reality*, Cambridge, MA: MIT Press, 1988.

Putnam, H., *Realism with a Human Face*, Cambridge, MA: Harvard University Press, 1990.

*Putnam, H., *Renewing Philosophy*, Cambridge, MA: Harvard University Press, 1992.

Putnam, H., 'Sense, nonsense and the senses. An inquiry into the powers of the human mind', *The Journal of Philosophy* 91/9, 1994, pp. 445–517.

Quine, W.V.O., 'Designation and existence', *Journal of Philosophy* 36/26, 1939, pp. 701–709.

Récanati, F., *Mental Files*, Oxford: Oxford University Press, 2012.

Reid, Th., *Essays on the Active Powers of Man*, in *The Works of Thomas Reid, D.D.*, edited by Sir William Hamilton, Hildesheim: G. Olms Verlagsbuchhandlung, 1983 [First Edition 1846].

Rorty, R., *Contingency, Irony, and Solidarity*, Cambridge: Cambridge University Press, 1989.

Rorty, R. *Solidarity or Objectivity?* (1984), in M. Krausz (ed), *Relativism: Interpretation and Confrontation*, Notre Dame, IN: University of Notre Dame Press, 1989, pp. 35–79.

Rorty, R., 'Charles Taylor on truth', in R. Rorty, *Truth and Progress, Philosophical Papers*, vol. III, Cambridge: Cambridge University Press 1998.

Rorty, R., *Truth and Progress, Philosophical Papers*, vol. III, Cambridge: Cambridge University Press 1998.

Scarpa, R., *Il caso Nuovo Realismo. La lingua del dibattito filosofico contemporaneo*, Milan-Udine: Mimesis, 2013.

Schelling, F.W.J., *Grounding of Positive Philosophy*, New York: SUNY University Press, 2007.

Searle, J., 'The campus war: a sympathetic look at the university in agony', 1971. www.ditext.com/searle/campus/campus.html [Accessed 4 April 2014]

Searle, J., *Making the Social World: The Structure of Human Civilization*, New York: Oxford University Press, 2010.

Smith, Barry., 'Document acts', *Proceedings of the Conference on Collective Intentionality*, Basel, Switzerland, August 23–26, 2010, available at http://ontology.buffalo.edu/smith/articles/documentacts.pdf

Strawson, P., *Individuals. An Essay in Descriptive Metaphysics*, Oxford: Oxford University Press, 1959.

Suskind, R., 'Faith, Certainty and the Presidency of George W. Bush', *The New York Times Magazine*, 17 October 2004.

Thomasson, A., 'Foundations for a social ontology', *Proto-Sociology: An International Journal of Interdisciplinary Resarch and Project* 18–19, 2003, pp. 269–290.

Varzi, A., *Il mondo messo a fuoco*, Roma-Bari: Laterza, 2010.

Vattimo, G. and Rovatti, P.A. (eds), *Weak Thought*, New York: SUNY Press, 2012.

VV.AA., *Storia dell'ontologia*, Milan: Bompiani, 2008.

Walton, K., *Mimesis as Make-believe: On the Foundations of the Representational Arts*, Cambridge, MA: Harvard University Press, 1990.

Wittgenstein, L. *Philosophical Investigations*, Oxford: Basil Blackwell Ltd, 1953.

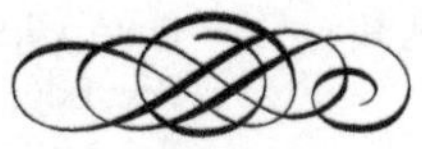

Index